THE LANGUAGE OF POETRY

The Language of Poetry

by

ROBERT MILLAR, M.A.

and

IAN CURRIE, M.A.

HEINEMANN EDUCATIONAL BOOKS

LONDON

Heinemann Educational Books Ltd
22 Bedford Square, London WC1B 3HH
LONDON   EDINBURGH   MELBOURNE   AUCKLAND
HONG KONG   SINGAPORE   KUALA LUMPUR   NEW DELHI
NAIROBI   JOHANNESBURG   IBADAN
EXETER (NH)   KINGSTON   PORT OF SPAIN

ISBN 0 435 10570 1

Printed in Great Britain by
Biddles Ltd, Guildford, Surrey

Contents

Acknowledgements

The authors and publishers wish to thank the following for permission to reprint copyright material: Jonathan Cape Ltd and Holt Rinehart and Winston Inc. for 'Neither Out Far Nor in Deep' by Robert Frost; Michael Baldwin and Longman's Green & Co for 'People' from *Death on a Live Wire*; The Trustees of the Hardy Estate and Macmillan & Co Ltd for 'At the Railway Station, Upway' by Thomas Hardy from *Collected Poems*; Macmillan & Co Ltd for 'Decomposition' by Zulfikar Ghose from *Jets from Orange*; Faber and Faber Ltd for 'Thrushes' by Ted Hughes from *Lupercal*, 'The Meadow House' by Theodore Roethke from *The Collected Poems*, 'A Study of Reading Habits' by Philip Larkin from *Whitsun Weddings*, and 'Mid-Term Break' by Seamus Heaney from *Death of a Naturalist*; Graham Hough and Gerald Duckworth & Co Ltd for 'A Newcomer' from *Legends and Pastorals*; The Society of Authors as literary representative of the estate of A. E. Housman, and Jonathan Cape Ltd for 'Epitaph on an Army of Mercenaries' from *Collected Poems*; Vernon Scannell for 'Incendiary'; Andrew Young and Rupert Hart-Davis for 'Passing the Graveyard' from *The Collected Poems*; R. S. Thomas and Rupert Hart-Davis for 'An Old Man' from *Song at the Years Turning*; Stevie Smith and Longman's Green & Co for 'Not Waving But Drowning' from *Selected Poems*; Peter Levi and André Deutsch Ltd for 'He met her at the green horse' from *The Gravel Ponds*; Mr Harold Owen and Chatto & Windus for 'Anthem for Doomed Youth' from *The Collected Poems of Wilfred Owen*; Norman MacCaig and Chatto & Windus for 'King of Beasts' from *Surroundings*; The Literary estate of Mervyn Peake and Chatto and Windus Ltd for 'The Cocky Walkers' from *Shapes and Sounds* by Mervyn Peake; Faber and Faber Ltd and Ted Hughes for 'You're' by Sylvia Plath from *Ariel*; MacGibbon & Kee for 'I thank you God' by e. e. cummings from *Collected Poems 1936–1962*; Iain Crichton Smith and Eyre & Spottiswoode Ltd for 'Rhythm' from *The Law and the Grace*; Laurie Lee for 'The Field of Autumn'; Donald Davie and Routledge and Kegan Paul Ltd for 'Thanks', Section V of 'After an Accident' from *Events and Wisdoms*; Mrs Ann Leslie Moore for 'How She Resolved to Act' by Merrill Moore; Mrs George Bambridge and Macmillan & Co Ltd for 'Gunga Din' by Rudyard Kipling.

Preface

This book is offered as an introduction in Practical Criticism. As such it deals with the language of poetry as a medium of communication, taking the view that poets are just people talking to other people. I. A. Richards, the originator of Practical Criticism, saw it as concerned with 'educational methods more efficient . . . in developing discrimination and the power to understand what we hear and read': an aim fundamental to good education and good English teaching.

Practical Criticism can thus be regarded as a valid discipline in itself. It can be more. No teacher of English today is likely to question the value of Creative Writing. But one of the difficulties in the educational use of Creative Writing arises from the need to provide some means whereby its exponents can expand and deepen their experience as well as develop their techniques of writing. Because Practical Criticism requires them to examine rigorously the products of minds more various, more subtle, more penetrating than their own, their world and their skills can be extended.

Moreover to anyone engaged in the teaching of poetry by the traditional method of teacher explanation it becomes increasingly more difficult to show poetic experience—of poet and pupil alike—as significant and relevant in everyday life. The pupil-centred nature of Practical Criticism has far more chance of revealing significance and relevance. And, if seriously undertaken, this approach to poetry can develop a personal critical awareness of the efficacy and the power of language, an awareness that will operate in other reading, thus giving a finer judgement about what is read and, very likely, a greater pleasure in the reading of it.

R. M.
I. C.

I

What Practical Criticism Works With

Der spring is sprung
Der grass is riz
I wonder where dem boidies is?

Der little boids is on der wing,
Ain't dat absoid?
Der little wings is on der boid!

Anonymous

It was a lover and his lass,
    With a hey, and a ho, and a hey-nonino,
That o'er the green cornfields did pass
    In the spring time, the only pretty ring time,
When birds do sing hey ding a ding ding:
Sweet lovers love the spring.

Shakespeare

Flushed by the spirit of the genial year,
Now from the virgin's cheek a fresher bloom
Shoots, less and less, the live carnation round;
Her lips blush deeper sweets; she breathes of youth;
The shining moisture swells into her eyes
In brighter flow; her wishing bosom heaves
With palpitations wild; kind tumults seize
Her veins, and all her yielding soul is love.

James Thomson

These are all, in their own way, expressive poetry or verse about spring. How they are different and what makes the difference and what judgement may be made of each is the business of Practical Criticism. Practical Criticism is a method for revealing to the reader-critic the total significance of the structure of words that is a literary work of art. In this book we shall think of the literary work in terms of poetry, and mostly in terms of short poems, or short stretches of poetry.

A poem, whether it be a long and involved piece of writing such as Milton's *Paradise Lost* or as short and straightforward as *Jack and Jill*, is a work of art, a structure in words, just as in their own way, using their own kinds of material, a statue and a cathedral and a symphony are works of art. And just as it is easy to tell that Coventry Cathedral is *different* from St Paul's, the Mona Lisa *different* from a self-portrait of Gauguin, Epstein's Genesis *different* from the Venus de Milo, an Elizabethan madrigal *different* from a Beatle's song, so it is easy to be aware immediately that Blake's *Tiger* is different from D. H. Lawrence's *Mountain Lion*.

CRITICISM AND CRITICS

All of us who are lucky enough to be able to read, see and hear are critics in the sense that with very little training or by just being exposed to different specimens of the same art, we can in a rudimentary way tell that one specimen differs from another; not only by subject matter but other qualities that we might find hard to define. We can tell there is a difference because the difference is there to be seen or heard, because each specimen is a unique kind of construction. We could tell, if the bonnets of a 'Jag' and a 'Mini' were lifted side by side, that the engines were different. To find the special construction, qualities and behaviour of the engine, how it was made, how it functioned and why it could do its work, we would require an expert in car engines—or possibly one of those car-daft boys who exist in any self-respecting school.

A famous professor of English, W. MacNeile Dixon, once said to a class of his honours students who were getting a bit uppity that an ordinary Ayrshire ploughman might well be a better critic of poems of Burns than *anyone* in his lecture room. He meant, of course, that the ploughman's immediate response might contain more of the right elements than even his best student's response. Everybody reacts in *some* way in reading a poem but even the right reactions or right feelings may be elementary and may not take us very far on the road to *understanding*. When you yourself merely react to a poem you as a critic are at the most primitive, though possibly enjoyable, stage of criticism. Yet we should remember the words of Charles Causley:

At the same time, the poem should conceal certain properties that may only reveal themselves very gradually. It's not the business of the poet to allow a poem, at a first reading, to burn itself out in one brilliant flash.

To travel beyond the first stage is to engage in a stimulating and instructive exploration into the mind of man. But it is necessary to know *how* to go further, how to make the exploration. And this is where Practical Criticism provides you with the means of doing so. Just as knowledge of the devices used in music deepens the estimation of Bach's *Jesu, Joy of Man's Desiring* so a knowledge of the devices of language used in poetry can contribute to a fuller, more perceptive judgement of a poem.

The basic kind of reaction, the simplest form of criticism is a response such as 'I like the poem' or 'I don't like the poem' or 'It doesn't do anything for me'. The number of factors that can cause the simple response can be varied. If supernatural poems give you nightmares you may at once dislike such poems. If you are sensitive to physical pain you may dislike poems that involve physical pain. Again, there are those who say 'Hands off' anything which has given them pleasure. They are quite content to let the words of the *Ode to a Nightingale* lap round them, enjoying their emotional reactions; as unthinking, though on a different art-plane, as those who revel in the unthinking ecstasy of a 'pop' song with psychedelic lighting— 'psychidyllic' as one pupil once wrote. But there are *kinds* of enjoyment as well as *degrees* of enjoyment. Through Practical Criticism you can refine and deepen your appreciation of the poet's art. You can appreciate him not just as the creator, transmitter and stimulator of feeling or truth or beauty or laughter or instruction. You can appreciate him as a meticulous artist in words, in patterns of words, in integrating and shaping thoughts. The reader at best can have a double bonus: enjoyment of first reaction, and an awareness of how the artist gives the enjoyment.

SOME ASPECTS OF THE PROBLEM

In any reading situation there are three factors to be taken into account. 1. The person who wrote. 2. The thing written. 3. The reader who is the interpreter. Let us consider in turn each of these factors that together make up a kind of chain of being.

The Person who Wrote

Any poem is a highly personal document created by a very complex being like you and me. He is a man of his own time, a thinking, feeling human being susceptible to all the experiences common to all men of all civilised ages known to us. But he is someone whose attitudes to and values about life are conditioned by the peculiar quality of the life around him. In the apprehending of the life within and around him he creates his poems. He tries to create something that is permanently true out of what is temporary and contemporary. Thus we today can to a certain extent recreate a poem written 5,000 years ago in Ancient Egypt, or 2,000 years ago in Greece just as we can recreate a poem written yesterday or last week.

So, when we come to read a poem we might want to know the private and public life of the man who wrote it, the historical background of his time, the kind of meanings words had at that time and so on. You can't appreciate fully Chaucer's *Prologue* or Pope's *The Rape of the Lock* without some knowledge of the society for which it was written or the beliefs and mental attitudes current at the time. Look up the word 'nice' in a good dictionary and you will find that it was a neutral term in one century, a term of abuse in another, and today it is complimentary. When Macheath, the original Mack the Knife, in Gay's *The Beggar's Opera* said to one of his girl friends 'Have you no bowels ?' the poet was not trying for a cheap laugh, nor was he enquiring about an indispensable part of her anatomy. He was merely asking that she have pity on his desperate plight.

But, in the end, as with a fifteenth-century painting, the poem must be able to be looked at as a work of art—in words. The 'meaning' of the poem has to come from the chosen words on paper and the kind of arrangement or pattern the poet has given them. And just as artists are recognisable by the way in which they choose to arrange their paint so poets are recognisable by the unique way in which they choose to arrange words. So that the trained mind can say 'This is the verse of Pope' or of Wordsworth or of Milton or of T. S. Eliot or Wilfred Owen. *How* they write is distinctive, personal and recognisable. Their personal trademark, their *style*, is merely their way of talking about aspects of life, of structuring in a texture of words their experience of what it is to be alive, and of transmitting it to an unknown reader. A poem is an act of personal communication, with words chosen to suit a variety of purposes, and the form of

4

the words so chosen has to be understood and appreciated if we are to get from the poem as much as possible of all the meaning intended by the poet. Most short poems, such as lyrics, take their rise from a rather chaotic mess of feelings and thoughts and perceptions. Out of this mess has to come order. Artistic creation is the process the mess has to go through as the poet decides the lengths of line, the kind of verse form, the patterns of words. In the end he has a finished piece of word construction that is his attempt to communicate all his experience as a human being to another human being. As Dannie Abse has it:

> Form, organisation, the decorum of style, alter the crude material until it is aesthetically acceptable to oneself as well as to others.

Or Philip Larkin in the same vein:

> Some years ago I came to the conclusion that to write a poem was to construct a verbal device that would preserve an experience indefinitely by reproducing it in whoever read the poem.

The Thing that is Written

From the person who did the writing let us turn to the thing that is written. Mostly we read poems, not with a large background knowledge of the poet but just for the poems themselves, these patterns of words, which we take to be self-explanatory even if sometimes difficult to grasp; not all artistry is easy. We have to think, in Practical Criticism, of the poem as a structure in itself, as an artistic artefact, like a painting, complete in itself. Of course, you can say it is easier to tell differences in painting, such as the kinds of colour used, but the fact that it may be harder to see differences in the use of words is no reason why we should not make the effort. It is certain that the effort will extend your knowledge of how language can be deployed, perhaps of how you yourself can deploy it: such effort will surely deepen and enrich your awareness of a poem, of poetry itself and perhaps give you added pleasure. The connoisseur of wine is a more dependable and understanding judge of wine than the happy-go-lucky swiller of quantities of plonk. And it is a connoisseur's taste in literature that your efforts can lead to.

You are not to be so naïve as to think of a poem that it has come to a poet in its entirety in a moment of inspiration. Those of you who do art will know that you rub out one line, put another in, add a detail, take it out again, try a colour, change to another colour. So with those of you who try to make a tune. Those of you who write poetry will know how frequently you use different combinations of words to get those that most satisfyingly express your thoughts and feelings. While we cannot explain how some patterns of words come complete from the poet's mind bearing the stamp of power, or how such patterns come to have the individual style of their creator, we *can* look at the words in front of us. Poets, and others, often agonise over the form of words that will convey as nearly as possible all that they are trying to express. This involves re-writing, deleting, inserting, changing the order of words until they have attained the final structure of words we know as a poem. It is not easy to find words that will say just what you mean. Flaubert, when writing *Madame Bovary*, agonised for days over the suitability of *one* particular word in his novel. T. S. Eliot refers to words as 'shabby equipment always deteriorating'. (Think of 'fabulous', 'smashing'.) Pope 'corrected and re-corrected' his poems till his dying day. So any poem we look at is liable to be the result of considerable thought, numerous changes, much deliberate manipulation of the poet's tools—his words. And even in the end he will not have been able to make his words say *all* that he wanted to reveal of the complex of thoughts and feelings that gave rise to the poem—that final pattern of words. This was why Paul Valéry said 'No poem is ever finished, only abandoned'. There is a value in knowing the skills that were employed to make the finished or abandoned product.

The Person Who Reads

The person who wrote. The thing written. Let us turn to the third factor, the person who reads. Each reader, by means of a pattern of black ink on white paper, re-experiences to some extent the original mood of the poet-writer. It's a kind of miracle of transmission. In one sense a poem exists as a pattern of words. In another sense it has no existence except when given an existence by someone in the act of speaking or reading it: then it becomes a re-creation of experience, subjecting the reader to various impressions.

But it would be wrong to believe that every reader of any one poem was 'reading' the same poem. People differ. They are of different ages: you will not see the same things in a poem at sixteen that you will at sixty. Each reader brings his own stock of knowledge, his own likes and dislikes, his own perceptiveness, his own degree of response to words. So in one sense every reading of a poem is a unique experience. This may help to answer a question your English teacher may have had to face: how he can go on reading the same poem or the same play year after year and yet still come to it each time as a new and fresh experience so that it has not lost its appeal?

Perhaps this is because of some of the qualities of poetry. It has been called 'A reading of life'. It is such a reading because, for the most part, the reader finds in poetry a confirmation of something he already knows, or else a revelation of some aspect he was dimly, perhaps not consciously, aware of, or else a preview of an experience he himself has not yet had. But whatever the poem yields to you, you will never get out of it *all* that the poet felt, divined, meant in using the words he did.

You bring your experience of life to interpret his experience of life. For example, in a certain emotional situation you may be content to say 'I love you'—perhaps the cliché of clichés in the English-speaking world. You use this as a 'blanket' term which the recipient can interpret according to the range of his or her acquired experience. In any situation the words may be simple but the reverberations they cause may be extensive. The world of poetry is filled with attempts to express what is implied in these three words, and in total these attempts provide an encyclopedia of shades and varieties and sub-divisions of love. Of course, if one of you comes upon a love poem your reaction might depend upon your immediate state: if you haven't been in love you may say 'Soppy': if you are in love you may react 'Super': if you have just become someone's 'ex' you may say 'Boloney!'

So we all react as individuals to the experiences common to all mankind. David Wright remarks:

> A good poem is a bit like a looking-glass. Nobody who picks one up is going to see the same reflection as the next man, for the simple reason that no two human beings—as yet—are identical.

You do react, nevertheless, as a person of your own time. Thus it is easier to find most immediate response to writers of your own time who use words, most likely, with the kind of meanings you yourself know. And the further you go back in time in English poetry the more difficult will it be for you to get *all* that the poet intended—though what you get may still be a great deal, even as far back as Chaucer. And in terms of Practical Criticism you may need to find out how words were used at the time before you can begin to see the poem as an artistic thing. Thus, if Practical Criticism is to be of value to you in developing your critical perception and producing more valid critical judgements on what you read, then we must realise there are limitations in what is presented to you. You should not be faced with poems without knowing who wrote them. For your criticism to be worthwhile you should not be unfamiliar with the cultural context. For you in school it is best to present you with texts from modern or comparatively modern works and writers. In such cases you have the chance of examining a text in the light of contemporary attitudes to life and the contemporary use of words. Moreover it would be valueless to present you with translations as a means of evaluating the work of a foreign poet.

You might want to discuss at this point whether you feel that Practical Criticism will spoil or enhance your enjoyment of poems. Is there any poem, for example, you can think of that you would not want to subject to a rigorous detailed scrutiny? You might also discuss what you get from a war poem if you have never had the experience of war, or what you get from an elegy if you have no direct experience of the death of someone near and dear to you.

YOUR SEARCH FOR TOTAL SIGNIFICANCE

The writer. The thing written. The reader interpreter. In Practical Criticism in this book you will be concerned almost entirely with the thing written and with yourself as the reader-interpreter. To help you, Practical Criticism provides you with a technique, a way of conducting your search for the total significance of a piece of poetry. How much of the total significance you can reveal will depend partly on the knowledge you bring and partly on the skill you acquire. Obviously, in the long run, the quality of your response will be decided by your own sensibilities and your own sensitivity to the nuances of language. There is therefore no substitute for wide reading among the best authors, which is, in the end, the way to acquire such sensitivity. But your ability to express your critical reactions to literature, and, for our present purpose, to poetry, can be improved if you are trained to know what to look for.

Thus in the remainder of this part of the book we shall be looking together at some aspects of the language that may be abstracted from any structure of words that is a poem. Of these aspects three are to be dealt with.

One is meaning. Don't imagine that what you will be looking for as the *total meaning* is what you think of as 'meaning' in the ordinary sense of the word, i.e., stating the ideas set down by the poet. 'Meaning' in that sense is only a part of the total significance. After all, consider for a moment some of the expressions available to obtain silence:

'Cease talking',
'Shut up',
'Belt up',
'Please be quiet',
'Give your vocal cords a vacation'.

The 'meaning' in the narrow sense of 'the action denoted by the words' is the same in each case. But the tone, the choice of words, the overtones and undertones of these words, would immediately be felt by you as part of the *total* significance of the utterance.

A moment's reflection will tell you that there are other factors which help to make up what we call 'meaning'. We convey our meanings by sounds or by symbols on the printed page that suggest sounds as we read. And it is a fact that different sounds and combinations of sounds can be used to have different effects on us. A baby will be calm for one set of sounds but be the reverse for another. The element of sound and what can be done with sound in English is something that must be scrutinised in any evaluation of poetic language.

A third element is that of grammar. Words have their own particular functions and have to be arranged in meaningful patterns before we can communicate effectively with others. Since many varieties of patterns can be constructed and yet make sense, it is clear that we must take account of how the chosen pattern contributes to the meaning of the utterances.

So the total significance of any poem is made up of a number of different 'meanings' which operate at different levels: the level of sound; the level of grammar; the level of meaning.

We must always remember, of course, that in reading, or at least in a first reading, all of those aspects of language tend to operate on us simultaneously. If we are very gifted, very lucky, very perceptive and very sympathetic, which few of us are, we may in the end be able to read a poem with something near to the whole response the poet intended us to have. Most of us have to settle for something much less.

We must also remember that no two poems will demand our attention to all aspects of language in the same proportion or to the

9

same degree. In any poem, it is for you, as critic, to decide how much attention you have to give to each in accordance with *what* the poet tells you and *how* he has chosen to tell it. Remember, too, that when you deal with a contemporary poet your judgements about his greatness are the judgements of yourself as a member of your own generation. Thomas Blackburn warns:

. . . 'Poet' is a posthumous word; you can't tell till he's very old or has been dead for thirty years or so whether you've had the genuine article or snappy ersatz number with a nylon back and plastic voice box.

But, even so, your judgements are more liable to be worthwhile if you have learned to look carefully and methodically at what poets do.

2

The Sound Element

It is not by accident that Tennyson, by the use of consonants, suggests firmness and hardness of eagle and rock in

> He clasps the crag with crooked hands

or Byron pokes fun at the sugar sweetness of writers of love songs through the consonants in the second line of

> When amatory poets sing their loves
> In liquid lines mellifluously bland

or Coleridge gives the feeling of the menace of sharp, arid heat partly through the short vowels in

> All in a hot and copper sky,
> The bloody Sun, . . .

or Tennyson conveys a sense of the ineffectual boredom of Ulysses' life through the long vowels of

> The long day wanes: the slow moon climbs: the deep
> Moans round . . .

Talking to each other day by day we are not concerned so much with the sound properties of the words we use, except at times when we employ intonation and stress. We are mainly concerned with choosing words to convey our meaning. And although the sound properties of words, singly and in combination, are not the most important aspects of poetic writing, the poet-craftsman finds that his ear is an indispensable part of his poetic equipment. As Brian Higgins observes in *To a Failed Poem*

> You are mysteriously diseased
> (Look at that wrong noise)

'noise' because the sound of the words is not right for what the poet wants to tell us.

How do we differentiate between the noises we make when

talking language? For without the power to give meaning to different sound combinations we would be restricted, like animals and birds, to communicating simple feelings by sounds that did their work by emotional contagion and were suggestions, for example, of alarm or anger. (Why can a whole play be conducted in mime?) At the most fundamental level we distinguish between such words as 'cat', 'sat' and 'mat' in the sentence 'The cat sat on the mat' because there is one sound in the combination of sounds that is different. For native speakers of English such as yourselves the habit of differentiating sounds and applying meaning to them is acquired so young that most of the time you do not need to think consciously about it. You spot quite easily when a mispronunciation or wrong combination is used. It is always vital in reading a text to make sure that the words you form in your minds are the words written by the author. In Practical Criticism we take it for granted that you do these processes correctly, and we can go on to deal with other aspects of sound that you may, but should not, take for granted.

Before doing so, we should point out that a writer can make use of the fact, usually for comic purposes, that confusions do arise through similarities in the sound of words. He may invent deliberate 'Malapropisms', as they are called. In a Malapropism instead of the right word another word of somewhat similar sound but widely different meaning is substituted. Of unintentional malapropisms we have heard in a bus queue 'I took my dog to the vegetarian surgeon'. In Sheridan's *The Rivals* Mrs Malaprop was of the opinion that a daughter should be taught orthography so that she would know the contagious countries and end by being a progeny of learning.

INTONATION AND STRESS

Your conversation with each other would be rather dull, as much reading of poetry and drama is dull, if all you conveyed was the dictionary or lexical meaning of the words you spoke. Part of the whole meaning of any spoken utterance may be given by facial expressions or bodily gestures (ask somebody to tell you what a spiral is), part is certainly determined by the patterns of intonation and by where you place the particular stress. You can turn a statement such as 'You're going to the concert' into a question by changing a falling pattern at the end into a rising pattern: or into a command by the stress pattern you give to the first words.

Let us first illustrate the importance of deciding the kind of sound pattern, and hence part of the meaning of what is written, by referring you to a play you are likely to know. Take *Macbeth*. At one point—and you can listen to what the Lady Macbeth makes of it in any production you go to see—any difference of intonation and stress conveys a difference of meaning. In a scene in which Lady Macbeth is making the final bid to force her husband to murder Duncan, she skilfully manoeuvres him to a stage at which he says, 'If we should fail?' The first sentence of her reply is 'We fail.' Imagine for yourselves the circumstances. Now, through the ways of saying 'We fail' see how many different meanings you can give the words, stating what you are trying to convey by each way. You can run the gamut from resigned despair to utter incredulity, from biting sarcasm to motherly comfort. One of the greatest actresses of this century simply said, in a flat voice, 'We fail.' Why?

In poetry it is just as necessary to read with the intonation and stress that will give the words their true meaning. Marc Connelly wrote, as his own epitaph, this:

> Here lies Marc Connelly.
> Who?

It is witty. It is also poignant as an epitaph for countless millions of the unremembered dead. What, do you think, should be the exact intonation given to 'Who?' if you want to bring out the wit and then if you want to bring out the poignancy? Again, Peter Redgrove, in *A Leaf from my Bestiary*, a poem about a worm working underground, says

> The fine grain at the grassroots stirs
> And his limy lips nibble in day—

the meaning of the second line being given by the stress and intonation of 'in'.

Take now lines everybody will have met;

> 'O where will I get a skeely skipper
> To sail this new ship o' mine?'

According to the metrical pattern there are for the words, 'I get', two possible stress patterns. You can stress 'I' or you can stress 'get'. Try to work out the differences in the king's situation and feelings by stressing one word then the other.

You can see from these examples how precision of meaning may have to be found from the stress and intonation. Almost all the lines of all the classic poems that you will read have stress and intonation closely inbuilt as part of their effectiveness and power. You have to read inferior poets or the masters in some of their off moments or off poems to notice any defects of this kind. If you want to see how this aspect of sound is handled with such superlative skill that stress and intonation seem inseparable from meaning read the first lines of Milton's *Paradise Lost*, a superb piece of language orchestration, or the Cockney pub-crawler woman's talk in section two of Eliot's *The Waste Land*, an impeccably adroit transformation of guttersnipe speech into fine poetry.

And if, in reading Wordsworth's *Simon Lee* or *Poor Susan*, your ear has not been troubled, look at them again to find Wordsworth in some of his 'half-witted sheep' moments. For example, apart from the unintentional ambiguity of 'tripped', what have you to say of the following line?

> Down which she so often has tripp'd with her pail.

Susan was simple. She was not so simple as the stress and intonation patterns of that line would suggest. Nor, mostly, was Wordsworth.

A very good example of an effect achieved by stress is a half-line from Ted Hughes' *Thrushes*, a poem which, since we shall refer to it frequently throughout this book, is printed below in full.

Thrushes

Terrifying are the attent sleek thrushes on the lawn,
More coiled steel than living—a poised
Dark deadly eye, those delicate legs
Triggered to stirrings beyond sense—with a start, a bounce, a stab
Overtake the instant and drag out some writhing thing.
No indolent procrastinations and no yawning stares,
No sighs or head-scratchings. Nothing but bounce and stab
And a ravening second.

Is it their single-mind-sized skulls, or a trained
Body, or genius, or a nestful of brats
Gives their days this bullet and automatic
Purpose? Mozart's brain had it, and the shark's mouth
That hungers down the blood-smell even to a leak of its own

Side and devouring of itself: efficiency which
Strikes too streamlined for any doubts to pluck at it
Or obstruction deflect.

With a man it is otherwise. Heroisms on horseback,
Outstripping his desk-diary at a broad desk,
Carving at a tiny ivory ornament
For years: his act worships itself—while for him,
Though he bends to be blent in the prayer, how loud and above what
Furious spaces of fire do the distracting devils
Orgy and hosannah, under what wilderness
Of black silent waters weep.

The half-line is that in which the poet describes the action of the
bird attacking a worm in the lawn:

> . . . with a start, a bounce, a stab

Here the combined effect of a very lightly stressed 'a' and the sharp
stress on the three short monosyllables 'start', 'bounce' and 'stab'
suggests the speed of three quick movements. It is noticeable that
many of the consonants are what we technically call 'plosives'.
These are formed by temporarily stopping the air flow from the
lungs and suddenly releasing it. Their use by Hughes reinforces the
idea of an abrupt (three plosives in that word) explosive release of
pent-up energy.

RHYME

Again at the level of sound, another device available to the poet
writing in English—classical Latin and Greek didn't use it—is the
device of rhyme. You must therefore train yourself, when the poet
uses rhyme, to notice what he is trying to achieve with different
kinds of rhyme or with different arrangements of rhyme. Ponder
for a moment over two stanza forms that are, according to the
traditional metrical system, basically the same in all respects except
that of rhyme arrangement. From Fitzgerald's *Rubaiyat of Omar
Khayyam*

Myself when young did eagerly frequent	A
Doctor and Saint, and heard great Argument	B
About it and about; but evermore	B
Came out by the same Door as in I went.	A

and from Gray's *Elegy*

> But Knowledge to their eyes her ample page   A
> Rich with the spoils of time, did ne'er unroll;   B
> Chill Penury repress'd their noble rage,   A
> And froze the genial current of the soul.   B

What different effects are open to poets who choose one or the other form of stanza?

As you can see, rhyme, the most obvious regular sound pattern in poetry, helps to structure ideas by linking lines together through similarities in the sounds of final words—strictly speaking, the final syllable or syllables, for you can have double or multiple rhyme. A *perfect rhyme* is present when the sound of the vowel and final consonant of syllables is the same, while the initial consonant or consonant cluster is different, e.g., mind and bind, charity and clarity, propriety and anxiety. Polysyllabic rhymes, often ingenious, are mostly used for comic purposes as by Butler in *Hudibras* or Byron in *Don Juan* or W. S. Gilbert in his 'patter' songs. Cleverly handled, they seem to introduce a sound element of grotesque exaggeration, as if parodying the serious use of normal rhyme.

Poets sometimes make use of internal rhyme. Up till this century it was almost always in the form of *middle rhyme* in which a word in the middle rhymes with a word at the end of a line as in this from Macauley's *The Battle of Naseby*

And the Man of Blood was there with his long essenced hair

The poets of the twentieth century are fond of using internal rhyme in much more subtle ways, as Auden in *Look Stranger*

The leaping light for your delight discovers

Now try to unveil the appeal of this very old poem which packs a number of rhyme features into its four lines:

> When Yule comes, dule comes,   (*dule,* sorrow)
> Cold feet and legs;
> When Pasch comes, grace comes (*Pasch,* pronounced as 'pace')
> Butter, milk and eggs.

There would seem to be a limit to the effectiveness of perfect rhyme as a linking agent. It does not normally operate upon us at intervals of much more than four lines: at longer intervals we tend to accept the line-ending as a sound on its own. Dylan Thomas in *Author's*

Prologue, a poem of 102 lines, constructed an elaborate rhyme scheme in which the first line rhymes with the last line, the second with the second last and so on. When you read the poem you are conscious of rhyme only in a few lines in the middle of the poem.

So far we have been thinking of perfect rhyme. But there are other possible patterns of sound that act as rhyme. Wilfred Owen used a device of linking lines by a form of rhyme in which the initial and final consonants provided the only resemblance. In *Strange Meeting* he has this strange rhyme:

> It seemed that out of battle I escaped
> Down some profound dull tunnel, long since scooped

Why does this kind of imperfect rhyme suit the image? Dylan Thomas on occasion had only the initial consonant of the last words of the line as rhyme. Another form of partial rhyme is called *Assonance*. In this there is the repetition of the same vowel but the consonant is different, e.g., race/fate. Still another form is that in which the consonant is the same but the vowel sound vaguely similar. Such, and other devices, are favoured by twentieth-century poets when they want some of the advantages of rhyme but not that exact correspondence which suggests unity or gives finality to the line ending. As Patricia Beer commented of one of her collections of poems:

> I greatly enjoyed using half-rhymes; they gave me much more satisfaction than full rhymes or none at all.

Since rhyme involves repetition of sound and repetitive sound has something of the compulsive hypnotic effect of incantation, poets are free to use the device in other ways as well. Captain Hamish Blair in his poem *Bloody Orkney* introduces the word 'bloody' forty-five times so that iteration robs the word of meaning. He thereby gains the effect, among others, of the automatic use of this and other oaths by the soldiery. Coleridge in *The Ancient Mariner* uses repetition to produce a kind of unreality in the reader, at the same time conferring a strangeness on a commonplace thing

> Water, water, everywhere,
> And all the boards did shrink;
> Water, water, everywhere,
> Nor any drop to drink.

Alliteration, too, can create linked patterns of sound for specific

17

purposes. (Indeed the poetry of our ancestors till the fourteenth century depended heavily on alliteration.) Look at it in Coleridge:

> The fair breeze blew, the white foam flew,
> The furrow followed free;
> We were the first that ever burst
> Into that silent sea.

A stanza of brilliant craftsmanship. The succession of stressed syllables with an initial 'f' is particularly appropriate to the image of the blowing wind, since the sound, known as a 'fricative', is made by blowing out air through partly closed lips. Notice, too, the internal rhymes of blew/flew, first/burst, the placing of the plosives, and especially the last eruption of movement by the sound of 'burst' before he finally becalms us with the last two sibilant words of the last line, ending in the long vowel of 'sea'.

One effective use of rhyme in a regular stanza is shown in Milton's *Lycidas*, an elegy. There is an irregular pattern of rhyme in almost the whole poem, suggestive of the chaos that death brings to the surviving, but the last eight lines are in the form of an *ottava rima*, the rhyme pattern of which is ABABABCC. The strict pattern betokens the return to calmness and normality, the restoration of order to life after mourning.

RHYTHM

Every poem is a rhythmical structure. Just because it is rhythmical it plays upon something fundamental in our nature. As A. E. (George Russell) has it:

> It is certain that metrics correspond to something in the soul.

We are conditioned by the rhythms of the world around us: the seasons, day and night, the waxing and waning of the moon, the birth, burgeoning and death of plants and pets. We ourselves live with our own rhythms: waking and sleeping, beat of the heart, breathing, eating and getting hungry. As rhythmical creatures we respond to rhythms suggested to us. We *impose* a rhythm of tick-tock on the unrhythmical tick of a watch. Now, have someone tap a pencil at regular intervals with the same force on a desk. How long is it before you impose a rhythmic pattern where there is none in reality? What are the prevalent patterns for the whole class? Having done this, consider how basic is the ballad stanza, the simplest of stanza forms, to the nature of man's rhythmic sense.

For a long time poets wrote under the idea that completely regular rhythmic patterns existed as the basis for their poetry. Such patterns were given special names such as iambic, trochaic, anapaestic, dactylic and so on. Each line contained so many 'feet' or units of the pattern and the arrangement of rhymes determined the names of forms in which they were composing. This, of course, provided a convenient method for describing what a poet was doing, and for showing where and how he departed from the basic metrical pattern.

But such descriptions do not carry us very far in Practical Criticism: we want to know something of the poet's intention in his use of patterns, the effect the pattern has in communicating to us and the place it has in the poem as artistic structure. Nowadays linguists believe that the rhythm of a poem is determined by an interplay of stress and vowel length. It is likely that the older view will be replaced by a scheme which sees the measure of the rhythm of verse as something akin to a bar in music, with an initial stressed syllable and a varying number of unstressed syllables. This way of looking at English poetry was first outlined by Gerard Manley Hopkins in a preface to a volume of his poems:

> . . . for purposes of scanning it is a great convenience to follow the example of music and take the stress always first, as the accent, or chief accent, always comes first in a musical bar.

At the moment, however, it would be best for you to look for the number of natural stresses in the line. So that, for example, instead of reading in traditional metre

The bóy stood ón the búrning déck

you would say

The bóy stóod on the búrning déck.

The importance of the interplay of stress and vowel length in establishing the rhythm of a poem can be easily observed by taking extracts from Milton's companion poems, *L'Allegro* and *Il Penseroso*, which are written in the same metre: whether it is iambic or trochaic, in the traditional terminology, is difficult to tell. For

19

most of *L'Allegro* the prevailing rhythm is fast, sprightly, almost jaunty as in

> Haste thee, Nymph, and bring with thee
> Jest and youthful jollity,
> Quips, and cranks, and wanton wiles,
> Nods, and becks, and wreathed smiles

You will notice that the syllables on which the stress falls are predominantly short. In the following lines from *Il Penseroso*, however, the syllables on which the stress falls tend to be long, giving a much slower, more stately and dignified rhythm:

> Come, pensive nun, devout and pure
> Sober, steadfast, and demure

Thus one of the things we have to do is to respond to the varying rhythms of poems and notice what they contribute to the total significance.

Some rhythms are far from subtle, and are used throughout the whole of a poem, whatever the ideas may be. Familiar to you will be the hoof-beat rhythm of Browning's *How they brought the good news from Ghent to Aix*, intended to suggest the galloping of horses:

> I sprang to the stirrup, and Joris, and he;

Similarly Louis Macneice in *Bagpipe Music* imposes the lilt and swing of one of a common kind of Scottish tune. The first stanza is

> It's no go the merry-go-round, it's no go the rickshaw,
> All we want is a limousine and a ticket for the peepshow.
> Their knickers are made of crêpe-de-chine, their shoes are made of
>   python,
> Their halls are lined with tiger rugs and their walls with heads of
>   bison.

If you care to look at Kipling's *Boots*, Hilaire Belloc's *Tarantella*, Vachel Lindsay's *General William Booth Enters Into Heaven*, or John Manifold's *Fife Music* you will encounter the same kind of usage.

But rhythms can be varied over a whole poem so that they are an important part of its architecture. In *Alexander's Feast* Dryden varies his rhythm to suit the successive themes of godlikeness, pity, wine, love and revenge. In *Night Mail* Auden, to suit the changing speed of the mail train as it crosses the Border into Scotland, changes the rhythmic speed of the verse while at the same time maintaining the rhythmic clatter of the train over the rails.

There are more subtle uses of rhythm, especially in twentieth-century poetry. Take again that half-line of Ted Hughes

> . . . with a start, a bounce, a stab

(try rearranging the order of 'start', 'bounce' and 'stab').

The monosyllables with their predominantly short vowel sounds make us increase the speed with which we say the words. Two lines later when Hughes wants to contrast the quick, decisive action of the instinct-obeying bird with human actions, he slows down the pace with polysyllabic words, full of consonant clusters—which are more difficult to pronounce—and with long vowels:

> No indolent procrastinations and no yawning stares,
> no sighs or head-scratchings.

In *Daddy* Sylvia Plath explores the love-hate, superior-inferior psychological relationship of daughter with father. She provides the feeling that part of her, in this relationship, is incurably and inescapably that of a child, and thereby makes an ironic contrast with the tragic implications, by adopting a rhythm that echoes the nursery rhyme. Linked to this type of usage of rhythm is that in which the deliberate use of specific rhythm is meant to make us think of the subject matter of a poem in which it was employed, as when, in this line of Eliot from *The Love Song of J. Alfred Prufrock*, we are meant to remember Browning's *A Toccata of Galuppi's*,

> For decisions and revisions which a minute will reverse.

MELODY

Rosemary Tonks said, in reference to one volume of her poems,

> My foremost preoccupation at the moment is the search for an idiom which is individual, contemporary and musical.

Immediately we think of 'musical' or 'melody' or 'melodious' we take them with the meaning of sweet and harmonious. In thinking of 'melody' as a feature of sound in poetry we have to extend the meaning of the word. We have to think of 'melody' as the fitness of a sound pattern to express the idea being conveyed to us. Just as the poet may have a subject or theme that is repulsive or distressing in actual life yet make it give pleasure through his poetic handling, so he may well use 'melodies' that, though they might be ugly to the ear, may give pleasure by their appositeness in the context of the thought and feeling at the time. So we may consider 'melody' partly in its normal sense but partly also as that music of words that fits best the poet's purposes.

First we must know the kinds of words the poet has at his disposal: three broad groups.

1. *Echoic or Onomatopoetic words*
   These are a rendering in speech of a variety of sounds. We imitate with 'cuckoo' or 'kook-a-burra'; birds caw, chirp and cheep; things click, crack or tinkle; humans sniff and wheeze.

2. *Symbolic words*
   In these the sound, though there is no direct imitation, and in some cases there cannot be, is suggestive of the ideas the words denote; as in see-saw, zoom, waddle, groan, slut, grudge, grouch. You may find it interesting to look in a dictionary at words beginning gr...., gl...., fl...., ch...., sl...., and sk.....

3. In the overwhelming number of words in the language the sound is in no way suggestive of the meaning: as in innumerable, bee, immemorial, elm.

When poets use the words of the first two groups it is easy for us to see how they are making melody. But the poet uses the third group also to create meaningful musical effects.

But even with this knowledge as part of our apparatus, the question of melody in verse is a perplexing one. Some poets use sound in such a distinctive way that we can recognise it as part of their poetic trademark. So that we can say that

> The stars of midnight shall be dear
> To her; and she shall lean her ear
> In many a secret place.

sounds like Wordsworth, or that

> Where palsy shakes a few, sad, last, grey hairs,
> Where youth grows pale, and spectre thin, and dies;

sounds like Keats. Yet it remains difficult to tell just why.

Nevertheless at least we know that any poet with all his known words available as his raw materials can prefer one to another, or one combination to another, because the sound will give him the effect he wants.

This aspect of sound makes it more difficult to engage in Practical Criticism of poems of the past. Language may have been spoken with different sounds at the poet's time of writing so that it is hard to estimate the result the poet intended. Let us illustrate this by a brief example from Pope's *The Rape of the Lock*. Poking fun at Queen Anne's inordinate fondness for liquor, he says:

> Here thou, great ANNA! whom three realms obey,
> Dost sometimes counsel take—and sometimes tea.

Apart from the meaning to be got from stessing the second 'sometimes' is there any difference to be had by pronouncing the words with something of the accent of a stage Irishman—as for example, 'tay' for 'tea'—as would have been the sound and melody in Pope's day? For such reasons we must be careful about judgements as to the imperfection of rhymes in older poetry. If you play in class records in which Chaucer or other poets are rendered in an imitation of how their language was spoken at the time of writing, you may discuss the effect on you.

If we may digress for a moment. As poetry has always been regarded as having an affinity to music, it could be interesting for you to look at how composers deal with the words of poets in setting them to music. You could take a Beatle's song, a song from a musical comedy, an aria from opera, a hymn, a famous poem or part of a famous poem such as the 'nightingale' excerpt from *Il Penseroso*. Or look at what Benjamin Britten does with Wilfred Owen's poems in *War Requiem*. You could think of the key that is chosen, how the notes and movement of the tune fit the words and the movement of the ideas. Then, if you are Scottish, or even if you are not, you could see what happens in Burns' songs, for he composed the poetry with the tune already in his head.

Under the heading of melody we may consider the device of onomatopoeia, where the sound echoes or reinforces the sense. Any given *sound* has no meaning in itself—how do Eh? Oh! M'm. come to have meaning? But when a sound is used in a given context, it may suggest the sense symbolised by the words or seem to enact the meaning, even although non-onomatopoetic words are in use. The poet may deal with the world of nature, as Tennyson in *The Princess*

> The moan of doves in immemorial elms
> And murmuring of innumerable bees

where the repetition of m's and l's suggests the drowsy drone of the bees as well as the sense of static peace.

Keats can deal with an inanimate object, as when he says of Autumn in the ode,

> Or by a cyder-press, with patient look,
> Thou watchest the last oozings, hours by hours

where the way in which we articulate the sound seems to reproduce physically the pressure on the apples.

Tennyson, again, in *A Dream of Fair Women* has lines on two human beings, Helen of Troy

> A daughter of the gods, divinely tall
> And most divinely fair

and Cleopatra

> A queen, with swarthy cheeks and bold black eyes,
> Brow bound with burning gold.

What is your idea of the qualities of the women from the different melodies of the lines?

Such examples are of euphonious 'melody'. But when Milton wanted cacophony to bring out the point of his idea he wrote in *Paradise Lost*

> Rocks, caves, lakes, fens, bogs, dens and shades of death.

or

> So he with difficulty and labour hard
> Moved on, with difficulty and labour he;

One linguist critic, Geoffrey Leech,[1] has analysed the opening lines of Coleridge's *Kubla Khan* in an effort to find the secret of their euphonious and compulsive magic.

> In Xanadu did Kubla Khan
> A stately pleasure-dome decree
> Where Alph, the sacred river, ran
> Through caverns measureless to man
> Down to a sunless sea.

Among the patterns of sound he noted that the rhyming word of every line is linked by alliteration to one of the words closely preceding it. Look for yourself what they are. In addition to the

[1] *A Linguistic Guide to English Poetry*, Longmans.

end rhyme there is an internal rhyme of 'pleasure' and 'measure' although they are separated by two lines. The first line contains a pattern of assonance on stressed syllables . . . and in the latter half of the excerpt there are a number of syllables all ending in 'n'. These patterns of sound, although they may not entirely explain all the music, certainly contribute to the musical quality of the lines. This becomes evident if we glance at the anonymous parody of the opening lines of *Kubla Khan*:

> In Bakerloo did Ali Khan
> A stately hippodrome decree
> Where Alf the bread delivery man, etc.[1]

METRICAL FORM

Having dealt with rhyme, rhythm and melody we are now in a position to think of the moulds in which poets may choose to cast their language communications.

First, there are whole poems whose metrical form dictates to the poet using them: laying down the metre, the number of lines, the pattern of rhyme and the length of lines. Of such are the sonnet, the triolet, the rondeau and the limerick. These forms impose severe technical demands on the poet, and you as critic will naturally look to see how far the restrictions are overcome or turned to advantage or how far they have provided a barrier to the expression of the thought.

Second, for the poet's selection there are a number of regular patterns, hallowed by custom and all with special names. These range from blank verse, which has no rhyme, through two-line forms of couplets to stanzas of various numbers of lines, lengths of line and rhyme schemes, culminating in the nine lines of the Spenserian stanza. In Practical Criticism it is not enough for you just to name them. You should already know what are the opportunities presented by each to the user, the dangers he can encounter. Take, for example, the Scotch or Burns stanza:

> But, Mousie, thou art no thy lane,
> In proving foresight may be vain:
> The best laid schemes o' Mice an' Men
> > Gang aft a-gley
> An' lea'e us nought but grief an' pain
> > For promis'd joy.

[1] Quoted in John Press, *The Fire and the Fountain*.

A few of the advantages offered are that it is admirable for conveying a simple intimacy, that the first three lines, all of the same rhyme, allow the close association of similar ideas or the contrast of ideas, that the last two lines permit the poet as an end remark to generalise, to make a dying fall, to make witty or serious comment, to surprise or startle by a new twist.

Your business, with each stanza form, is to try to observe the kind of purpose the poet has in using it, the various ways in which he bends it to suit his thought.

And whenever a poet invents a stanza form, you ought to probe the question of why he has adopted this arrangement of lines. Just one instance. In *To a Skylark* Shelley has this:

> Hail to thee, blithe Spirit!
> Bird thou never wert,
> That from heaven or near it,
> Pourest thy full heart
> In profuse strains of unpremeditated art.

To anyone who has watched, and listened to a lark, it is clear that the stanza is meant to suggest something of the flight pattern of the ascending skylark and also something of the pattern of its song.

In the present century, although stanza forms are still frequently used—many of them invented—the predominant poetic form is the one known as *Free Verse*. The poet in Free Verse is at liberty to adopt throughout his poem whatever line lengths he wants, in any line whatever rhythmic patterns he wants. Although generally without rhyme he may use some rhyming devices somewhere. The poem thus becomes a structure of the exact length demanded by the subject, patterned in sound and rhythm according to the demands of each individual idea as well as to the overall demands of the poem as a whole. A formidable task. Don't imagine that good Free Verse is easier to write than good verse of the traditional kind. It is not. It imposes the severest of trials on the ear of the poet. Free Verse poems will ask of you the closest attention if they are to reveal the part played by the sound element in their total significance. You should remember that in Free Verse it would seem that the natural tendency is to make each line consist of a single image. If you take this as the norm, you can then notice where and how the poet departs from it and can form some estimate of his aim in so doing.

POETRY HEARD AND POETRY PRINTED

So far we have been dealing in this chapter with poetry as sound, the substance of language. Indeed poetry existed first only as sounds in the air and ear, and all languages have or have had poetry as part of their oral tradition. Think of the extensive body of English and Scottish ballads. In Chaucer's day poetry was read aloud to an audience or to oneself and even after the invention of printing it was a century or two before the practice of silent reading was customary.

Nowadays poetry is normally read silently, perhaps in the privacy of your own room. The fact that it is printed, that it is available to be gone over again and again has led to its becoming more and more complex, too difficult to grasp through the ear alone. It is a task to listen to a Shakespeare play if you do not know the text beforehand, it is tantalising to listen to poetry on T.V. or radio. Yet there are signs today among young poets, as there was among the 'take poetry into the pubs' poets of the 1930's, that they are thinking along the lines of restoring the immediate oral appeal of poetry, with poetry readings to large audiences and the institution of festivals of poetry and jazz.

In the opposite direction to the tradition of spoken verse, there has developed that type of verse known as *Concrete Poetry*. Concrete poetry deliberately exploits the opportunities given by the printed page. Since any poem printed has a visual shape, words might be so arranged as to create a visual impact, and different colours might be used for printing, or different colours of paper to put the print on. Some poets have therefore written poems that are not recognisable as poetry other than in visual terms. But while writers of concrete poetry are concerned with what the visual shape will do to the reader, some are able in addition to exploit the time factor in reading. Thus they obtain unusual effects by utilising the time it takes for the reader's eye to travel across space from one word to another or by positioning understandable words in apparently abnormal places.

Such poets are, of course, merely extending to its limits what poets have done in the past through line lengths, line endings and punctuation. In the seventeenth century religious poets shaped their poems into the visual form of hour-glasses, triangles and in our own day Dylan Thomas, in one clever use, the form of a Holy Communion wine-cup. Moreover the placement of words in a space relationship has been an element in much Free Verse this century. e. e. cummings, the American poet, in his simple little poem, *Just Spring*, runs the names of children together—eddieandbill, bettyandisobel—as a single word to indicate, perhaps, that the two persons are inseparable, and the arrangement of the final phrase

> far
> and
> wee

with a separate line for each word suggests the sound of the balloon man fading into the distance.

Look at this poem by e. e. cummings. We give you the clue that it is extremely difficult to see a grasshopper in grass and that the grasshopper only becomes visible at the last line.

                    r-p-o-p-h-e-s-s-a-g-r
                who
       a)s w(e loo)k
       upnowgath
                PPEGORHRASS
                                    eringint(o-
    aThe):l
            eA
                !p:
    S   a
                        (r
    rIvInG   .gRrEaPsPhOs)
                                        to
       rea(be)rran(com)gi(e)ngly
       ,grasshopper;

The authors of concrete poetry, however, can construct their poems from the beginning as patterns of words arranged upon the page to form shapes which convey significance, a significance which perhaps could not be conveyed in any other way or at least not so economically. Many of the modern concrete poems could be regarded as amusing verbal jokes. Edwin Morgan, for example, has a short poem which is presented in the following form:

> Pool!
> Peopl
> eplop!
> cool.

Obviously the form describes with great economy people diving or jumping into a pool to cool themselves, but our attention is drawn to the odd separation of the final 'e' in people and its transfer from the end of the second line to the beginning of the third line. We notice, however, that this ensures that the third line contains exactly the same letters as the second but arranged in a different order. If the letters had been arranged in the order lpoep, the third line would have been an exact reflection of the second line. As it stands, is it too fanciful to interpret the line as indicating the distorted reflection that people would see gazing into a pool, or perhaps people diving in higglety-pigglety: or their cries of enjoyment, or all three?

Now try to apply to the following short extracts the information you have had in this chapter on various aspects of sound.

Exercises—Sound

1. The flower
            fallen
    she saw it
            where
    it lay
        a pink petal.
                            William Carlos Williams: *The Loving Dexterity*

2. He lunges for the stair, swings down—off,
    Into the sun for his Easter eggs,
    on very
        nearly
            steady
                legs.

                            Edwin Morgan: *Good Friday*

3. The students drowsed and drowned
    In the teacher's ponderous monotone—
    Limp bodies looping in the wordy heat
    Melted and run together, desks and flesh as one
    Swooning and swimming in a sea of drone.
                            Colin Thiele: *Bird in the Afternoon*

4. It's Coming—the postponeless Creature
    It gains the block—and now—it gains the Door.

                    Emily Dickinson: *It's Coming*

5. His mighty work for the Nation
    Making peace and strengthening Union
    Always at it since on the throne:
    Saved the country more than a billion.

                    Anonymous

6. I am otherwise I know;
    Many books have made me sad:
    Yet indeed your stately slow
    Motion and its rhythmic flow
    Drive me, drive me, drive me mad.

                    Harold Munro: *At a Country Dance in Provence*

7. Then old man's talk o' the days behind' e,
    Your darter's youngest darter to mind 'e;
    A li'l dreamin', a li'l dyin';
    A li'l lew corner o' airth to lie in.

                    Eden Philpotts: *Man's Days*

8. Booth led boldly with his big bass drum.
    (Are you washed in the blood of the Lamb?)
    The Saints smiled gravely and they said: 'He's come'.
    (Are you washed in the blood of the Lamb?)

                    Vachel Lindsay: *General William Booth Enters into Heaven*

9. One morning in spring
    We marched from Devizes
    All shapes and all sizes
    Like beads on a string.

                    John Manifold: *Fife Music*

10. When mountain-surges bellowing deep
    With an uncouth, monster-leap
        Plung'd foaming to the shore.

                    Coleridge

11. O O O O that Shakespeherian Rag—
    It's so elegant
    So intelligent
    T. S. Eliot, The Waste Land

12. It was a high day, a crisp day,
    The clearest kind of Autumn day
    With brisk intoxicating air, a
    Little wind that frisked, . . .
    Richard Eberhardt: The Soul Longs to Return Whence It Came

13. The fact
    That a drop
    Of water
    Throws shadows
    Or, rather,
    A focus
    Of dark on a wall
    In its fall
    Is enough for terror:
    Michael Baldwin: The Water-Butt

14. Signposts whitened relentlessly.
    Montreuil, Abbeville, Beauvais
    Were promised, promised, came and went,
    Each place granting its name's fulfilment.
    Seamus Heaney: Night Drive

15. In the deep of the dark when the mid-night is gone
    And the quick pulse of life falls solemn, and soft, and slow;
    When the spirit a moment keeps pause in the urge of its flow,
    I wait for my sleep time and lie as under a stone.
    William Soutar: In the Deep of the Dark

3

The Grammatical Element

As we have already said, the whole 'meaning' of any stretch of language is conveyed in a number of different ways. What can be contributed by sound we have looked at in some detail. But when we communicate with each other, a more important factor in determining what we mean is the grammar of the language. We shall think of grammar here as the different types of words we use and the kinds of meaningful patterns into which we arrange them; always remembering that poets allow themselves much more freedom for their purposes than do writers of prose.

WORDS IN THEMSELVES

When we learn a language, it is not enough, as you well know from your efforts with a foreign language, simply to acquire a vocabulary. We must also know the different forms words can take and how they are strung together in the accepted patterns of the native speakers. In English we could learn all the half million or so words in the Oxford Dictionary but still be unable to communicate, except in the most primitive or infantile way, unless we knew the grammar of our language.

First we must remember that all words belong to word-classes; they are grouped, according to usage, into nouns, verbs, adjectives, adverbs, prepositions and so on. And we must remember the ways in which words are formed. Other foreign languages known to you still have numerous inflected forms, i.e. they change their endings according to the grammatical function they perform or the gender of the words they accompany. English has largely lost such inflections, only a handful remaining in the noun, pronoun and verb. Because there is a limited number of forms of each word the English language is, for poetic use, a very flexible instrument. You need look for very few unusual grammatical features that are significant in our poetry, especially twentieth-century poetry. Among them, however, may be noted the following:

32

1. *Archaic Forms*

The obsolete forms of the second person singular of pronoun and verb—still commonly found in religious usage—may still be met with. In older poetry they were often used to suggest familiarity or to intensify the sense of desire. They can still be used to give the flavour of the past where the context is suitable. Wherever they crop up in otherwise contemporary language we have to ask ourselves why they have been used and what is gained by their use. As, for example, when Dylan Thomas in *Why east wind chills* has the line

> When cometh Jack Frost? the children ask.

He thus connects the modern child with children of past ages, seeing them as alike in their questing minds.

Similarly with other occasional archaic forms of the verb, such as subjunctive forms, or, for example,

> Swifter be they than dappled dreams.

2. *Shift of Word-class*

This deviation occurs when the poet shifts a word from its normal word-class and uses it in a different role. Shakespeare was especially noted for allowing himself great freedom in this way. It is still a device used by poets to effect surprise, endow their language with novelty, or give a new significance to an idea. There is a well-known instance in Keats, *Ode to Autumn*. 'Plump' is usually an adjective but Keats uses it as a verb:

> To swell the gourd, and plump the hazel shells
> With a sweet kernel;

The word aptly conveys the idea of the growth of the nut towards its round shape.

Let us look at a related trick of language used by the American poet e. e. cummings (what is the effect of his writing his name that way?). A great deal of the apparent obscurity in his poetry is clarified if we realise that cummings had the habit of replacing words of one word-class with related words in another word-class. For instance in his poem which begins

> Pity this busy monster, manunkind,
>
> not.   (what about 'manunkind'?)

he uses the phrase 'curving wherewhen'. A little thought about the context makes clear that he is referring to Einstein's relativity concept of a space-time continuum but has replaced the nouns 'space' and 'time' by the corresponding adverbs of place and time 'where' and 'when'. Again in his poem 'Anyone lived in a pretty how town' (make sense of that title) he has a line:

he sang his didn't he danced his did

Obviously 'didn't' and 'did' are used as members of the noun word-class. The sense of the line can be teased out if we substitute the meaning of 'achievement' or 'accomplishment' for the notion of 'did'. Thus 'didn't' becomes 'what he did not succeed in achieving' and 'did' becomes 'what he succeeded in achieving'. So we understand by the line that he took his failures and successes in life equally lightheartedly; basically not, perhaps, an original idea, but made memorable by the originality of its wording.

Now talk about the following examples from contemporary poets:

They took away the water-wheel,
Scrap-ironed all the corn-mill;   —Patrick Kavanagh.
They midge him round   —John Holloway.
Kisskissing his servants' hands in agony—Thomas Kinsella.

5. Compounding of Words

In poetry one very interesting aspect of word formation is likely to be the poet's use of compound words. Of course the practical demands of everyday life make such compounding a recognised feature of English as may be seen in such words as hitch-hike, sun-bathe, timetable or lipstick; after all, few people would think of connecting 'lips' and 'stick' if a new object had not demanded a new name. But the poet in his creation of compound words fuses together two ideas, obtaining surprise and compression, to form a novel poetical concept.

You can see this kind of creation particularly well in the poems of Gerard Manley Hopkins, an indefatigable experimenter in poetical techniques and a prolific coiner of compound terms. In *Spring and Fall*, a poem describing a child grieving for the leaves falling from the trees, he says that as the child grows older she will not

spare a sigh
Though worlds of wanwood leafmeal lie;

34

The coinage 'wanwood' conveys economically the stark desolation of the denuded trees by combining a word applied to the human world (and, especially, ill children) with one from external nature. 'Leafmeal' by analogy with 'piecemeal' suggests the random fall of the leaves one by one and their scattered, bit by bit, mealy appearance on the forest floor.

We can notice the same economy, surprising union, and new force in the use of the adjective 'rollrock' in his poem *Inversnaid*.

> This darksome burn, horseback brown,
> His rollrock high road roaring down.

Try now, these:

> Down by the Forum a blind-fingered fiddler.
>
> > Charles Causley
>
> to uncover my ego-plundered eye.
>
> > Dannie Abse

At this point we take a brief look at another way of utilising words as grammatical features. It is the unusual splitting of words by placing part of the word at the end of a line and the remainder at the beginning of the next line to bring out some new aspect of meaning, as in Patrick Kavanagh's

> Him, him, the ne'er-
> Do-well a millionaire.

or e. e. cummings's

> un
> der fog
> 's
> touch

SYNTAX

Turning from single words in grammar we may now consider what grammarians call syntax, the arrangement of words so that they make meaningful statements. Each language has its own peculiar conventional patterns of word order, and a sentence can rarely be translated word for word into another language. Errors of sentence pattern appeal to our sense of humour (Shakespeare used the device in *Henry V* with the French Princess and with the Welshman,

Fluellen). Writers of farces may make a German use English words with a German syntactical pattern: 'I have today my book forgotten . . .' A Huguenot pastor exiled in England once chose as a text for his sermon 'The devil goeth about like a roaring lion, seeking whom he may devour'. He caused some consternation among his English congregation when he announced that he would divide his discourse into three heads, 'who the devil he is, where the devil he is going, and what the devil he is doing'.

The normal pattern of the grammatical elements in English is Subject, Predicate, Complement (including direct and indirect objects) Adjunct (adverbial modifier) as in 'He kicked the ball into the goal'. In T. S. Eliot's *Whispers of Immortality* we find the sentence

> The crouched Brazilian jaguar   S
> Compels the scampering marmoset   PC
> With subtle effluence of cat.   A

Much of the effect Eliot obtains comes from the isolating of the parts of the sentence in his line arrangement. Incidentally, what completion do you normally expect after the verb 'compels' and what does Eliot attain by his completion with an adjunct?

Not all of these four elements need be present, of course, and occasionally a poet will make use of the simple combination of Subject and Predicate for the sharpness and precision with which it makes impact and for the isolation of an idea, as Tennyson does in *The Brook*.

> I slip, I slide, I gloom, I glance,

or D. H. Lawrence in *Mountain Lion*:

> They hesitate.   SP
> We hesitate.   SP

The next two lines of the same poem add the third element:

> They have a gun.   SPC
> We have no gun.   SPC

The poet may, and usually does, depart from the normal S.P.C.A. order, or complicates it in some other way, although contemporary poets tend to use the normal order more frequently than those of earlier ages. (Can you suggest why?) Considerably more freedom has always been allowed to the poet than to the prose writer in varying the normal grammatical patterns of English. This is explained partly by the poet's having to contend with the exigencies of metre and rhyme. Many astonishing examples can be cited, but just one from the Scottish Metrical Psalms will be enough.

> I with my groaning weary am,
> I also all the night my bed
> Have caused for to swim; and I
> With tears my couch have watered.

Mostly, however, the skilful poet is able to triumph over such difficulties and utilise his variations to enhance our experience of what he is communicating. *Elegy Written in a Country Churchyard* is often criticised because of the unoriginality of its ideas and the monotony of its tone, yet it remains an attractive poem. Part of the attraction comes from the skill with which Gray uses deviations from the normal S.P.C.A. order. Examine this stanza closely:

> Oft did the harvest to their sickle yield,
>   Their furrow oft the stubborn glebe has broke;
> How jocund did they drive their team afield!
> How bowed the woods beneath their sturdy stroke!

Would you like, too, to decide for yourself whether Lovelace has triumphed in the second of these two lines from *To Lucasta, Going to the Wars?*

> I could not love thee, dear, so much
> Lov'd I not Honour more.

WAYS OF THROWING EMPHASIS

1. *Variation of Syntax*

We have said that the poet rarely puts sentences in their normal order of parts. But these liberties he can take with syntax also provide him with a powerful aid to the transmitting of more than the narrow 'meaning'. Just as many modern painters do not obey the traditional 'grammar' of painting but put a nose in one part of the canvas, three eyes in another part and so on, so poets may not feel obliged to obey the orthodox grammar of their medium, language, in their efforts to put down most tellingly what they want to express.

You will therefore need to look closely at any poem to find out how the poet arranges the grammatical units of his sentences. Where the poet's sentences are long, consisting of more than one clause, this may be difficult, for the possible variations are so numerous, but if you learn to take each clause in turn you will gain some insight into what he is effecting. We shall content ourselves here with some simpler but skilful examples of variation.

Notice how the change of word order in the opening line of Ted Hughes' *Thrushes* throws emphasis:

Terrifying are the attent sleek thrushes on the lawn, CPS

Here the normal order has been varied. This highlights the opening word of the poem, and this colours and conditions our attitude to the ideas of the remainder of the poem. Similarly, when Hughes begins that section of the poem in which human activities are contrasted with those of the thrushes, he introduces it with the sentence

With a man it is otherwise. ASPC

By moving the adjunct 'with a man' to the beginning he has related the thrush to man and insured that what follows is seen as in contradistinction to what has been said about the birds.

Two interesting ways of throwing emphasis through syntax occur in one arrangement of the simile and in the figure of speech known as Transferred Epithet. In the simile the poet frequently puts the part beginning with 'like' or 'as' first:

Like as a father pitieth his children
So doth the Lord pity them that fear him.

In this case the inversion of the parts of the simile allows the simpler and more familiar idea to be presented first, the more profound part being then more easily understood. In the transferred epithet the adjective that really applies to one noun or pronoun is so placed as to appear to apply to another. In

The ploughman homeward plods his weary way

the poet manages to relate the ploughman more closely to the path which he is taking and heightens the sense of tiredness.

We may mention here, too, that you should look out for the differences in the lengths of the sentences poets write, for length, as well as structure, may be of significance. We can again illustrate this from *Thrushes*. The first stanza which describes the instinctive automatic reactions of the birds opens with a longish sentence, but using a straightforward simplicity of structure in its parts—two sentences are without finite verbs at all. In the last stanza, however, the complexity of the situation of human beings is reflected in the complexity of structure of the long sentence that forms the bulk of the stanza. In Eliot's *Sweeney Among the Nightingales* we find each of the first two 4-lined stanzas is a sentence in itself. The remaining eight stanzas, 32 lines in all, is a single sentence. In it the great number of varied images and ideas are to be regarded as interacting with one another to form a single complex.

2. *Parallelism*

Just as a feature of the poet's use of sound is the recurring pattern, so the recurring pattern is often a feature of the syntactical organisation of a poem or part of a poem. The triolet depends for its effect not only on a recurring syntactical pattern but on the recurrence of the same words that make up the pattern. Indeed the recurrence of syntactical pattern is so important that we shall look at its uses in some detail.

One of the simplest uses is that form of repetition known as *Anaphora*, in which the poet uses the same word or words as the opening of a number of successive lines of his poem. We find in Keats' poem *Isabella*

> And she forgot the stars, the moon, and sun,
> And she forgot the blue above the trees,
> And she forgot the dells where waters run,
> And she forgot the chilly autumn breeze;

The girl, Isabella, has had the gruesome experience of secretly digging up her murdered lover's body and she has cut off and retained the head, as a treasured memento of her love for him. She is about to go mad. The anaphora accentuates the gradual but inexorable quality of her declension into madness, the piecemeal dissolution of her contact with and making sense of the real world, her isolation within the confines of her own disordered mind and imagination.

What do you think the syntactical parallelism contributes to this little piece of comic misanthropy by Sir Walter Raleigh, *Wishes of an Elderly Man at a Garden Party?*

> I wish I loved the Human Race;
> I wish I loved its silly face;
> I wish I liked the way it walks;
> I wish I liked the way it talks;

And when I'm introduced to one
I wish I thought *What Jolly Fun*!

A simple but memorable example occurs in Tennyson's *The Charge of the Light Brigade* in which he magnifies the danger and magnifies the courage by the pattern of

Cannon to right of them,
Cannon to left of them,
Cannon in front of them

For a more elaborate, but yet easily observable use, let us turn to a poem you will all know, John Masefield's *Cargoes*. The sentence structure is very simple. Each stanza consists of a single minor sentence (without a finite verb); there is a noun group followed by a participial phrase and a prepositional phrase. What is the significance of this identity of syntactical structure? Each stanza deals with a trading vessel at different times in history, the times of ancient Nineveh, renaissance Spain, and modern Britain. In each stanza the kind of vocabulary changes, the sounds and rhythms imitative of the vessels' different movements change, and thus we are given a sense of the alterations through time. But the unchanging sentence pattern of each suggests the unchanging human activity of the men who go down to the sea in ships.

A final example, in which the use is subtle and elaborate, is Dylan Thomas' *The Force that through the Green Fuse Drives the Flower*. We shall choose some points that are not too difficult.

The force that through the green fuse drives the flower
Drives my green age; that blasts the roots of trees
Is my destroyer.
And I am dumb to tell the crooked rose
My youth is bent by the same wintry fever.

The force that drives the water through the rocks
Drives my red blood; that dries the mouthing streams
Turns mine to wax.
And I am dumb to mouth unto my veins
How at the mountain spring the same mouth sucks.

The hand that whirls the water in the pool
Stirs the quicksand; that ropes the blowing wind
Hauls my shroud sail.

And I am dumb to tell the hanging man
How of my clay is made the hangman's lime.

The lips of time leech to the fountain head;
Love drips and gathers, but the fallen blood
Shall calm her sores.
And I am dumb to tell a weather's wind
How time has ticked a heaven round the stars.

And I am dumb to tell the lover's tomb
How at my sheet goes the same crooked worm.

Let us look carefully at the first two lines of stanzas 1, 2 and 3. Each has the same syntactical pattern: 'The force' + the 'that' clause + a verb + a complement. And in each of the stanzas this pattern is followed by a parallel construction such as 'that blasts the roots of trees'—S.P.C.—but with a contrasting meaning. The first structure in each case deals as to its meaning with the forms of life growth or activity in the natural world and in man, the second structure with the forces of death and destruction. Don't be put off by the apparent deviation from the rigid formula of meaning in the phrase 'stirs the quicksand'. It is not really a deviation. Thomas has incorporated a pun in 'quicksand' intending 'quick' to be taken in its older sense of 'living' (as in 'the quick and the dead') and 'sand' as in 'the sands of life'. The juxtaposition of nature and man is thus maintained.

Thus, partly by the syntax, Thomas has shown the unity of the natural forces that operate, so that behind them seems to be a single compulsive principle; he also has united nature and man in one general scheme of creation and destruction.

At the beginning of stanza 4 he abandons the syntactical parallelism as he develops his thought in a new direction. But he retains some connection between this and the other three stanzas by keeping the parallelism of the third lines of each, drawing added strength from the actual repetition of 'And I am dumb'. The final couplet, then, is related to everything that has gone before by the same opening words and the same syntactical structure. We have looked at only *one* feature of the poem. It has many other features which, when you have finished this part of the book, you might care to explore.

It is worth noting that two figures of speech take their effectiveness from their syntactical arrangement. One is *Antithesis* in which two ideas are balanced against or contrasted with each other as in Pope's line

> To err is human, to forgive divine.

and

> Youth is full of pleasance,
> Age is full of care.

The other is *Chiasmus* in which the second part of the antithesis is arranged in an order the reverse of that of the first, as in

> Walk in thy light, and in thy temple bend.

In each case you will need to look further than syntax, to evaluate the choice of the balancing or contrasting terms.

3. *Condensing or Ellipsis*

When considering sentence structure we have always to remember that the poet has extra freedom in manipulating language, not only by arranging the order of the parts of sentences to suit his purpose, but also by choosing to omit words. The kinds of words that he can omit are what are known as non-lexical items, i.e. words that do not carry meaning. Some of these may be essential connections which the reader may have to assume are present. Their omission can bring into sharper focus the imagery of the poet and can allow of a compressive force. Often these may be obtained at the expense of clarity, or at least of clarity in a first cursory reading, for the meaning can be teased out. One short example is from Auden's *Prologue*, where the omissions are further complicated by the unusual sentence structure:

> Alive like patterns a murmuration of starlings
> Flying in joy over wolds unwittingly weave;

Another is the second line of this pair from Peter Redgrove's *Dialogue in Heaven*:

> Why should he live at all?
> Madam! the feelings!

Hopkins often requires you to supply some of the minor familiar words. In one of his sonnets he writes

> O the mind, mind has mountains; cliffs of fall
> Frightful, sheer, no-man-fathomed. Hold them cheap
> May who ne'er hung there.

In addition to the difficulties made by any other devices, the word 'those' must be understood before 'who' in line 3, so that the sentence in prose order becomes 'Those who ne'er hung there may hold them cheap'. See, too, how Wilfred Owen in *Dulce et Decorum Est* achieves a sense of desperation and frantic activity by omitting 'There was' before 'An ecstacy of fumbling' which, as it stands, is not syntactically connected to the next line:

> Gas! Gas! Quick, boys!—An ecstacy of fumbling,
> Fitting the clumsy helmets just in time.

Thereafter he reverts to complete sentence patterns for his next purpose of a return to orderliness.

Now try to tease out the sense of this stanza from Dylan Thomas' *Poem in October*. There may be more than one way of filling in the gaps so that it becomes grammatically acceptable, or, of course, you could consider whether it is grammatically acceptable as it stands.

> It was my thirtieth year to heaven
> Woke to my hearing from harbour and neighbour wood
> And the mussel pooled and heron
> Priested shore
> The morning beckon
> With water praying and call of seagull and rook
> And the knock of sailing boats on the net webbed wall
> Myself to set foot
> That second
> In the still sleeping town and set forth.

4. *The Company Words Keep*

It is one of the characteristics of language that individual words tend to be found frequently, some of them normally, in association with certain other words. These collocations as they are called have been exemplified by a famous linguist, J. B. Firth, who pointed out that the word 'ass' will often be found with 'silly' or 'stupid' and it is more likely to be modified by 'young' than by 'old'. Similarly the word 'time' is likely to be found in conjunction with such verbs as 'spent', 'passed', 'wasted' or 'frittered away'.

But the very fact that we thus form habits of expectation gives the poet innumerable opportunities to surprise, shock and delight us. Whenever we meet words in unfamiliar company we are drawn up short. And as poets are trying to convey the unique quality of their

experience they tend to express themselves at times through fresh
or less usual combinations of words. We are therefore frequently
surprised, sometimes captivated, often forced to ponder the meaning.
A new shaft of light is directed on life or some familiar aspect is
presented in a stimulating guise.

This is the basis of the figure of speech known as *Oxymoron*, in
which there is an apparent contradiction between related words, or
the *Paradox* in which the statement at its surface value seems to be
absurd but on closer examination is seen to make sense. In Dryden's
Alexander's Feast we have

> The vanquished victor sunk upon her breast,

where the unusual combination serves to bring out the 'power of
love and the power of the music that induced the love. Wordsworth
in *The Rainbow* startles us with

> The Child is Father of the Man.

A powerful example of unusual association is found in Yeats'
Easter 1916 in which to end three of his verses he uses the line

> A terrible beauty is born.

The juxtaposition of 'terrible' and 'beauty' is unusual enough to
make us consider the implications of the sentence and we are
shocked into an awareness of the repulsion-fascination the rebellion
had for the poet: we also become alive to the two ways in which the
two sides taking part might look at the same action.

We have presented you with extreme examples of words keeping
unusual company. But you should always be on the alert to notice
them even in lines that seem straightforward, as in these from W. J.
Cory's *Heraclitus*

> Had tired the sun with talking and sent him down the sky

In stretching usages to their limits twentieth-century poets are fond
of the device known as *synaesthesia* in which there is a kind of cross-
fertilisation through the unusual union of two or more senses. They
do this by associating, let us say, a word from the area of sound
perception with a word from the area of sight perception, as in 'a
pale moan', 'the scarlet blare of a trumpet'. Peter Redgrove opens
his *Dialogue in Heaven* with

> A round, hollow, laughing silence,

Derek Mahon opens his *Bird Sanctuary* with

> Towards sleep I came
> Upon the place again,

and you can contrast 'Towards sleep' with the time clause in the line from Tennyson's *A Dream of Fair Women*

> I read, before my eyelids dropt their shade.

The best known phrase of this kind is Dylan Thomas's 'a grief ago'. In it he associates human feeling and time in an unusual way. We would normally expect a noun denoting time before 'ago'. Nevertheless the meaning is perfectly clear and the fresh combination serves to accentuate the idea that life is lived, not from one day to another, but from experience to experience.

In *Fern Hill* he uses a perhaps more unusual variation in the phrase 'once below a time'. This is not just a linguistic perversity. It points up the significance of the theme, apart altogether from its capacity to surprise us. *Fern Hill* describes the young boy happy in the enjoyment of the natural world and blissfully unaware that he too shares in the general human predicament—he must grow old and die. As he is thus subject to the ravages of time, so 'once below a time' is more appropriate than the hackneyed 'once upon a time'. Thomas has given new meaning by the conversion of an inert phrase, while retaining the innocence implied in the original. In the same poem he uses 'all the sun long' and 'all the moon long' instead of 'day' and 'night'. In this case he emphasises that for the young boy time was not measured by mechanical means or by the routines of the workaday world but by the effect upon him of the heavenly bodies he could see and which were an experience to him.

Now try to apply to the following short extracts the information you have had in this chapter on the various aspects of the grammatical element. You can also, of course, make use of what you have learned about aspects of sound.

Exercises—Grammatical Element

1. Annihilating all that's made
   To a green thought in a green shade.

   Marvell: *Thoughts in a Garden*

2. I lighted down my sword to draw,
     I hackéd him in pieces sma',
     I hackéd him in pieces sma',
       For her sake that died for me.

Anonymous

3.   jeez ja see dat skirt
      did ja glom dat doll!
    who was telling you we wuz brudders.

Carl Sandburg

4. All shuffle there; all cough in ink;
     All wear the carpet with their shoes;
     All think what other people think;
     All know the man their neighbour knows.

W. B. Yeats: *The Scholars*

5. You ask a poet to sing
     Why
     Even the birds are hoarse.

Alan Bold: *Recitative*

6. Through which he had wandered deliciously till he stumbled
    Suddenly finally conscious of all he lacked.

Louis Macneice: *The Suicide*

7. Its town house furniture
     had an on-tiptoe air
     of waiting for the mover
     on the heels of the undertaker.

Robert Lowell: *For Sale*

8. Twilight. Red in the west.
     Dimness. A glow on the wood.

John Masefield: *The Wild Duck*

9.   So, Prince, you suggest that I've bolted my shot?
     Well, like what you say, and soul your damn!
      I'm an upple litset by the talk you rot—
     But I'm not so think as you drunk I am.

J. C. Squire: *Ballade of Soporific Absorption*

10. In June, amid the golden fields,
    I saw a groundhog lying dead.
    Dead lay he; my senses shook.
                    Richard Eberhardt: *The Groundhog*

11. Just when I seemed about to learn!
        Where is the thread now? Off again!
    The old trick! Only I discern—
        Infinite passion, and the pain
    Of finite hearts that yearn.
                    Browning: *Two in the Campagna*

12. But here will sigh thine alder tree
        And here thine aspen shiver:
    And here by thee will hum the bee
        For ever and for ever.

                                Tennyson

13. For the sword outwears the sheath,
        And the soul wears out the breast
    And the heart must pause to breathe
        And love itself have rest.

                                Byron

14. I wake up with a headache, chew all day
    Aspirins, go to bed dispirited,
    Still with a dull pain somewhere in my skull,
    And sleep. Then, in my dreams, the sun comes out.
                    Philip Hobsbaum: *Astigmatic*

15. What if a dawn of a doom of a dream
    bites this universe in two,
    peels forever out of his grave
    and sprinkles nowhere with me and you?
            e. e. cummings: *What if a Much of a Which of a Wind*

The Element of Meaning

'When I use a word,' Humpty Dumpty said, in a rather scornful tone, 'it means what I choose it to mean. Neither more nor less!'

'The question is,' said Alice, 'whether you can make words mean so many different things.'

'The question is,' said Humpty Dumpty, 'who is,to be master, that's all.'

In our search for ways of attaining to the total significance of a poem we have looked at the part that can be played by sound and by grammar. The element we are now going to discuss—the 'meaning' of the words used—is the most important of all. Obviously the poet's prime task is so to use words that, when we read what he has written, we can understand the meaning. Only if we understand are we in a position to begin our criticism, to assess the poet's achievement. Apart from infrequent and odd vagaries of language usage, whenever we find poetry hard to understand it is rarely because the actual words are unfamiliar to us or their normal meaning is too difficult. It is usually because they are used by the poet in an abnormal way.

WHAT IS 'MEANING' OR THE UNIQUENESS OF WORDS

Right at the outset we had better be sure what we mean by the 'meaning' of words. On the surface this would seem to be an absurdly simple question. You may dismiss it by saying that the 'meaning' is the definition supplied by your dictionary. If it is one of the best dictionaries you would frequently find not one meaning but several, in some cases a great number; and some of them very different from each other. The commoner a word is, the more often it is used in speech and writing, the more 'meanings' it is likely to acquire.

If you look at the big Oxford English Dictionary you will find that you can use 'come' in 69 different senses, 'go' in 94, and 'make' in 97. The Thorndike Word List records words not alphabetically, but in the order of the frequency of their occurrence. The total number of different meanings given, with examples of use, in the Oxford English Dictionary for the first 500 words in the Thorndike list is 14,070, an average of 28 for each; and the average for the 1,000 words most frequently used is 25.

Thus, although your dictionary will give supposedly equivalent words, there are no such things as synonyms except in dead phrases such as 'last will and testament' or 'by use and wont'. We have to regard every word in the main word-classes of noun, verb, adjective and adverb as unique—and any word used as having only an approximate meaning to any other word given as its dictionary equivalent, even although both may represent the same idea.

In the first place words do not have a meaning on their own, in isolation, but in a *verbal context*. The meaning we attribute to any one will be determined by the kind of context in which we find it. For example, the word 'man' has different meanings in the following sentences: in

Man was made to mourn

'man' means the species, man, or if we might so put it, in this instance 'man' embraces 'woman'. In

The Child is Father of the Man

it means 'adult'. In

The *Mermaid* rocked to hear the man

it means the person—Shakespeare. In

When lovely woman stoops to folly
And finds too late that men betray,

the plural of 'man' is used to differentiate between the two sexes, whereas both were included in the term 'man' in our first sentence above. In certain verbal contexts there may be no human connotation at all, as in a game of chess or draughts

He had only one man left on the board.

Now work out for yourselves the meaning in this phrase from *Vitae Lampada*, a poem referring to a school cricket match, 'and the last man in'; and in the question 'Call yourself a man?'

In discovering which of the meanings in the dictionary fits a particular use we are helped by the context in which we find it.

There are subtle shades of difference in the contexts in which words can be appropriate, for words carry with them other kinds of significant attributes. To the careful deployer of words, such as a poet, or even to the not so careful deployer of words, such as ourselves, the words 'girl', 'damsel', 'lass', 'bird' and 'floozie' are not interchangeable.

Verbal contexts apart, there is the kind of *situational context* to which the words apply. Thus if a writer has golf as his situation, or we are playing on a golf course, or it is a golfing scene in a novel or play, such words as 'slice' or 'shank' or 'eagle' or 'birdie' are more likely to refer to things in the game.

Even in the narrower, strictly 'notional' view of meaning, you have to be careful when you are reading the poetry, but more often the prose, of other English speaking peoples, or of dialect writers within Britain. For example you would need to be sure, when you met them in American writing, of words such as robin, yard, corner, gas, block, candy, or cookies, to take only a few.

Moreover we have to be aware that there may be other aspects of meaning with which the poet has intentionally loaded the words he has selected. Words have other kinds of associations than the strict lexical meaning in the particular age in which they were used. Some have been dirtied, some have been made commonplace, some have been specialised, some made ridiculous or made to sound pompous. They carry with them our social reactions and our linguistic experiences. To substitute another word for 'lass' in Shakespeare's description of Cleopatra 'a lass unparalleled' is to rob the phrase of its unique qualities.

Words therefore might be said to refer to 'areas' of meaning and the exact point in the area of meaning is determined by the context.

AMBIGUITY AS A POETICAL DEVICE

It can be, of course, that it is difficult to decide which of the various possible meanings of a word the author intended. In prose this could usually be a fault, since the prose writer is expected to choose and arrange his language so that he makes his precise meaning clear. But there can be times when the poet may want to make his statement carry more than one meaning, or be capable of more than one interpretation—as in the prose of the Delphic oracle of old, or today's fortune tellers.

One simple example of this is the *Pun*. In a pun, when the same sound or sounds are made, or reproduced in our inner ear from the printed page, we are supposed to be conscious of the implications that arise from there being more than one meaning to the word in its context. Take the well-known instance of the bride's description of her forthcoming wedding. 'Aisle! Altar! Hymn!' In poetry the pun is normally reserved for comic purposes as in Thomas Hood's *Faithless Nelly Gray*:

> But a cannon-ball took off his legs,
> So he laid down his arms!

or, of a boy dying from swallowing mercury, the anonymous

> 'Twas a chilly day for Willie
> When the mercury went down.

But in serious poetry of the twentieth century the pun is also being used, sometimes with strong or subtle effect. A. M. Klein in *Filling Station* uses the word 'lyric' in two senses with telling power in

> (Beyond the hills, of course,
> the oxen, lyric with horns, still draw
> the cart and the limping wheels.)

You may notice, in passing, how the poet uses brackets to remove us from the busy road and transport us to the depth of the countryside.

Again, estimate what is gained by the pun in this line from Dylan Thomas's *Do not go gentle into that good night* (is there a pun in 'good night'?)

> Grave men, near death, who see with blinding sight

Another figure that depends on ambiguity of meaning is *Innuendo*. In this the words are so chosen and arranged that we are intended to take an additional meaning from them. For example Abel Edwards had this to say of a man of considerable girth and tonnage:

> When Tadlow walks the streets, the paviours cry,
> 'God bless you, sir!' and lay their rammers by.

What did Pope imply when he presented a dog to His Highness the Prince of Wales and had an inscription on the collar, which he knew courtiers would read?

> I am His Highness' dog at Kew;
> Pray tell me, sir, whose dog are you?

or Ogden Nash in the second of these lines in a poem on females wearing trousers

> You look divine as you advance—
> Have you seen yourself retreating?

A third figure that depends on meaning is *Irony*. When this is used we are expected to take exactly the opposite meaning to one or more of the words written as in the later phase of Antony's speech in *Julius Caesar*

> For Brutus is an honourable man.

But there are other occasions in serious poetry when the poet may enrich his verse by deliberately writing so that a number of different meanings may be held in tension while the implications of all of them are vaguely felt. You may find that even the simplest looking poem may have subtleties of this sort within it, as William Empson shows in the following stanza from a very old anonymous poem:

> Cupid is winged and doth range,
> Her country so my love doth change;
> But change she earth, or change she sky,
> Yet will I love her till I die.

Here 'change' may mean 'move to another' or 'alter the one you have got' and 'earth' may be 'the lady's private world' or 'the poet's world' or 'the world at large'. It is not necessary to exclude any of these meanings, as we would be tempted to do in prose writing.

Such ambiguities of meaning afford the poet effects that, in terms of the meaning of the verse, are somewhat analogous to the effects he can achieve on the level of sound by imperfect rhyme. They do occur frequently in the Free Verse of twentieth-century poets because of the lack of punctuation or because in the presentation of images there is withheld from the reader the grammatical information necessary for interpreting the stretch of language as a clear statement. Yeats in *Leda and the Swan* has this line:

> He holds her helpless breast upon his breast.

Does the adjective 'helpless' modify the preceding pronoun 'her' (or even 'he') or the succeeding noun 'breast' or does it refer back and forward at the same time?

HIDDEN 'MEANINGS' OR THE SUPRA-INFORMATIVE PROPERTIES OF WORDS

Although the prime function of lexical words is to convey the notional meaning, most of such words, especially when used in poetry, can be made to do other work as part of their total meaning. Words can be used not only to denote or to describe the world outside us and the world within. We can, by our specific choice of the words open to us, convey how we feel about such things. Words, in addition to the information they supply, may have an emotive quality, carry an emotive charge, can have undertones and overtones of feeling that they have acquired in the course of their sometimes long history. Some words are almost entirely emotive. 'Nice', 'lovely', 'beautiful', 'horrid', 'pleasant', 'repulsive' and many others beloved of advertising men, or vogue words such as 'fabulous' or 'smashing' do not really give us information about the things they are applied to. They mainly tell us about the feelings or reactions of the people using them. When Philip Larkin writes in a poem 'Get stewed' there is little, if any, lexical meaning intended: it is the feeling that is conveyed by the vulgar colloquial expression.

In using the word 'vulgar' just now we introduced another aspect of words, related to and often inseparable from the emotive aspect. We can use words so that we make judgements. Such words carry an evaluative quality within them. We may use them to express praise or blame, or admiration, or other attitudes of mind. To take an outlandish instance: to be called a 'Red' in the United States, or in some social and political circles in Britain, is to be abused; to be called a 'Red' in some other countries or some other political circles is to be praised. Often part of the force of a simile or a metaphor may reside in some judgement that is involved in the comparison. If, of all the words available for a dwelling place the word 'hovel' is used in 'like a hovel' then the word carries the judgement that the place is mean and sordid as well as the feeling of disgust or, depending on the context, perhaps pity. If an American poet refers to a place as a 'joint' this term implies he regards it with disfavour. None of us, it is hoped, would refer to a girl for whom we have respect as a 'bird' except where we intended it to carry flippant or facetious or affectionate overtones rather than derogatory ones.

These examples show how different words carry different emotional charges or different evaluative judgements, or both together.

But it is possible to express the same idea in words that suggest approval, disapproval, or neither. An Income Tax Inspector, for example, apart from the metaphor 'bloodsucker' might be referred to approvingly as 'a public servant', disapprovingly as 'a bureaucrat' or neutrally as 'a civil servant'. Try using 'dog' in these ways. It is this flexibility in use that lies behind *Euphemism*, in which a harsh reality is put in a pleasing form of words, as in W. S. Landor's

> I warmed both hands before the fire of life;
> It sinks, and I am ready to depart.

It also lies behind the figure of speech known as *Circumlocution*, in which an idea is expressed in a roundabout way, as when, instead of saying 'toothache' we say 'hell of all diseases' or as when Gray, instead of saying 'swim' says

> to cleave
> With pliant arm, thy glassy wave

But it is not only the kind of feeling and judgement that may come from the selection of words. The intensity of feeling and judgement may vary too. It is often possible to choose the appropriate one from an assembly of words that can be arranged in a sort of scale of increasing or decreasing approval or disapproval. A thin person's reactions to your language might be different according to whether you called him/her slender, scrawny, lissom, stringy, scraggy, skinny, slim. Do you agree with this scale: buxom, plump, stout, overweight, Junoesque, fat, obese? There is certainly no mistaking the venomous disapproval in Hermia's name-calling of the tall Helena 'You painted maypole, you!'

The same word even may have a different emotive charge in different contexts. Compare 'sweeting' in Shakespeare's

> Trip no further, pretty sweeting,
> Journeys end in lovers' meeting—

with the same word in Ogden Nash's

> Sure, deck your lower limbs in pants;
> Yours are the limbs, my sweeting.

The word 'home' for example, has a strong potential emotive charge which is released in lines such as 'Home, sweet home' or 'For England, home and beauty', 'Home is the sailor home from the sea' (think too of the word 'country' or 'land'). T. S. Eliot in

The Waste Land cleverly uses the emotive charge of the word by using it seriously at first and then in an ironic way.

> At the violet hour, the evening hour that strives
> Homeward, and brings the sailor home from sea,
> The typist home at teatime, clears her breakfast, lights
> Her stove, and lays out food in tins.

'Home' of course can be quite neutral as in The Home Service or The Home Office. You could try devising emotive and non-emotive contexts for 'academic', 'suburban', 'provincial'.

Just how the poet may exploit the 'colour' of words to create atmosphere you can easily see in the opening lines of Keats' *Ode to a Nightingale*

> My heart aches, and a drowsy numbness pains
> My sense, as though of hemlock I had drunk,
> Or emptied some dull opiate to the drains
> One minute past, and Lethe-wards had sunk:

You will notice how Keats reinforces the idea of 'drowsy numbness' with such words as 'pains', 'hemlock', 'emptied', 'dull opiate', 'drains', 'Lethe(wards)' and 'sunk', all suggesting destructiveness or possible death, or the ending of things.

Similarly Tennyson creates a feeling of lassitude, but a different kind from that of Keats, in *The Lotus Eaters*:

> In the afternoon they came unto a land
> In which it seemed always afternoon.
> All round the coast the languid air did swoon,
> Breathing like one that hath a weary dream.
> Full-faced above the valley stood the moon;
> And like a downward smoke, the slender stream
> Along the cliff to fall and pause and fall did seem.

Having given a special meaning to 'afternoon' by writing 'always afternoon' he reinforces it with such words as 'languid', 'swoon', 'weary', 'dream' and 'pause'. We are here concerned only with the 'colour' given by words. Obviously in all cases the sound and the rhythm combine with the meanings to produce the total effect. (If you like, take the Tennyson extract and analyse the lines separately, in particular getting out just how the rhythm of the last two lines contributes to the sense.)

Some words, 'damsel' is one, take their tones from the contexts or the environment in which they were used, and which help to determine the contexts in which they will release their emotive charge. Note how redolent of the age of romance and chivalry the word 'casement' is as compared with the more humdrum counterpart 'window'. Hence its fascination for Keats and hence his use of it in special contexts:

> Charm'd magic casements, opening on the foam
> Of perilous seas, in faery lands forlorn.

or

> Full on this casement shone the wintry moon
> And threw warm gules on Madeline's fair breast.

The importance of the 'colour' of words has been aptly illustrated by C. H. Thouless, who has translated the last two lines thus in colourless terms:

> Full on this window shone the wintry moon
> Making red marks on Jane's uncoloured chest.

The objective facts, or 'information', remain the same but all the poetry and romance have evaporated.

THE FITNESS OF WORDS FOR POETRY

Notions that certain words are fit or not fit for use in poetry, or are better fitted or less fitted, change from age to age. Dryden said that Spenser wrote no language, because of the peculiarity of his vocabulary. Shakespeare and his contemporary playwrights used almost everything that came to hand. The attitude of the poets of the eighteenth century could be summed up by two of Gray's statements 'The language of the age is never the language of poetry' and 'Our poetry has a language peculiar to itself'. Wordsworth led a return to simplicity of syntax and vocabulary, as he thought, and twentieth-century poets seem to regard all language, and some non-verbal means of communication such as arithmetical figures, as capable of poetic use. We are not now, as in the eighteenth century, likely to be tossed on the 'main' by a 'billow' while the 'finny tribe' swim beneath, nor are we likely to be 'swains' and 'maids' sung to by 'feathered choristers' while 'zephyrs' blow over scenes of 'gore'.

At that time, too, the poet was allowed to use certain contracted words to help him in his struggle with the demands of strict metre. Words like "'Tis' or 'e'er' or 'e'en', the stock-in-trade of poets were not likely to be found in the conversation or the prose of the time.

With the swing of the pendulum, and under the influence of T. S. Eliot, you are liable to find nowadays words drawn from almost any variety of the language. Words are not right or wrong in themselves, they are fit or not fit according to the context in which they appear, and their success in meeting the purposes for which the poet uses them. Thus we find words formal and informal, colloquial, vulgar and regional dialect. And these may be mixed together in the same poem, a selection and a procedure that would have made earlier poets hold up their hands in horror.

T. S. Eliot has no hesitation, in *Triumphal March*, in putting down

> 5,800,000 rifles and carbines,
> 102,000 machine guns,
> 28,000 trench mortars,
> 53,000 field guns.

or Alan Bold in *Sir Humphry Davy*, where Coleridge is imagined as saying

> Can it help me write good poetry?
> No! and what's the use, old son,
> Of sodium, potassium, calcium,
> Barium, magnesium, and strontium?

or Alan Bold again, in *A Memory of Death*, has

> William Bold/Clerk of Works/ (Dept. of Agric. for Scot.)/
> ...1956/March/Found drowned in Bigbreck Quarry,/
> Twatt, Birsay, about 4.30 pm. on Sunday 18th /March
> 1956, Last seen alive, about 6.30 pm. on/Wednesday 14th
> March 1956.........

If you take the point of such examples, you will be prepared to accept whatever kind of language communication the poet chooses and look at it for its fitness and its effect in context.

You will find too, especially in twentieth-century poets—among them Eliot, Pound, Lawrence and Rupert Brooke—the introduction into the English text of words or phrases or whole sentences from some foreign language. An example from an earlier poet is taken from Browning's *Soliloquy of the Spanish Cloister* in which Latin is used with ironic intent:

> Blasted lay that rose-acacia
>   We're so proud of! *Hy, Zy, Hine* . . .
> 'St. there's Vespers, *Plena gratia*
>   *Ave, Virgo!* Gr-r-r- you swine!

Another feature, increasingly prevalent, is the use of quotations from other poets or other books. This occurred in older poets, particularly in the incorporation of phrases from the Bible or, in the eighteenth century, the inclusion of snippets translated from classical poets. Such quotation may be simple as in Byron's

> The road to hell is paved with good intentions

but may be in its purposes and effects very complex as in Pope or Eliot. You must be careful to notice just how the quotation is introduced and what, in the context, the poet seems to be trying to make it do. In *Why Patriots Are a Bit Nuts in the Head* Roger McGough incorporates a snatch of a sonnet by Rupert Brooke, and the poem cannot properly be understood unless we know the Brooke poem:

> if you have your belly shot away
> and your seeds
> spread over some corner of a foreign field.

Often, too, the quotation may be used to achieve an effect contrastive with the situation in which it first occurred: a simple example is Wilfred Owen's use of *Dulce et decorum est pro patria mori* in the last lines of *Dulce et Decorum Est*:

> The old lie: Dulce et decorum est
> Pro patria mori.

or Eliot's use of an altered version of a line by Goldsmith in *The Waste Land* when we are meant to think of the original poem:

> When lovely woman stoops to folly and
> Paces about her room again, alone,
> She smoothes her hair with automatic hand,
> And puts a record on the gramophone.

FIGURES OF SPEECH

Among the resources of language open to the poet are those that collectively have come to be known as 'Figures of Speech'. And, in the study of poetry, they have hypnotised teachers and taught into more absurd antics than any other aspect of poetic technique.

Nobody with any pretensions to finding out just what poets and poetry do should become like Miss Groby, the school teacher at whom James Thurber pokes fun because she brought 'the fierce light of identification' to the study of English Literature. In Thurber's words,

> She was forever climbing up the margins of books and crawling between the lines, hunting for the little gold of phrase, making marks with a pencil. As Palomides hunted the Questing Beast, she hunted the Figure of Speech. She hunted it through the clangorous halls of Shakespeare and through the green forests of Scott.
>
> Night after night, for homework, Miss Groby set us searching in *Ivanhoe* and *Julius Caesar* for metaphors, similes, metonymies, apostrophes, personifications, and all the rest. It got so that figures of speech jumped out of the pages at you, obscuring the sense and pattern of the novel or play you were trying to read.

(Notice, incidentally, how Thurber here parodies the learning he got through Miss Groby.)

Don't, like Miss Groby, ever be led into the error of thinking that because you can tell what figures of speech a writer uses that you have made a meaningful statement about him. To say that Shelley in *Ode to a Skylark* uses brilliant similes and metaphors or that the eighteenth-century poets used apostrophe, personification, antithesis, inversion, etc., is to reveal nothing. You might as well say that George Best or Pele or Jimmy Johnstone are great footballers because they wear football boots. Devices of language are the common garb of poets, and figures of speech just one part of the garb.

What is important is that you are able to appreciate what impact a particular figure of speech has, what function it performs in the poem, how it is used by the poet to get the response he wants from the reader, how it helps him to give his special quality to the experience he is trying to communicate. While it is obviously helpful—as a kind of shorthand method—to recognise some of the commoner figures of speech, you can very well be affected by such devices without knowing they are there, and you can very well see, on a closer scrutiny of the text, how the poet achieves a particular effect without being able to give the technical name to the language device he is using. For example it so happens that Thomas Campbell uses *Repetition* in the following line:

Again, again, again and the havoc did not slack.

What is important is to notice that each 'again', with the accent on the second syllable, suggests another crash, of guns obtaining a crescendo effect and intensifying the sense of destructive power. By *Repetition* Tennyson achieves just the opposite kind of effect, a diminution of power, a descent into nothingness, as each individual echo is suggested by 'dying' with the accent on the first syllable:

Blow, bugle—answer echoes, dying, dying, dying.

Although it is difficult to classify some figures of speech, basically they fall into two different types; those which depend for their effect on the arrangement of words, and those in which the meanings or the associated ideas of words are brought into play.

Figures of Arrangement depend on the patterned arrangement of words and we have noticed some of them already. Normally the pattern is determined by some logical principle. In general such figures are useful for highlighting or emphasising the poet's presentation of his thought. But he can do much more. In *Climax* ideas are arranged in ascending order of importance. Look how Leigh Hunt in *Rondeau* manages to convey his scale of values in life as well as his own situation and at the same time pay a gracious compliment to Jane Welsh Carlyle in this climax,

Say I'm weary, say I'm sad,
  Say that health and wealth have missed me,
Say I'm growing old, but add,
  Jenny kiss'd me.

In *Anti-climax* ideas are arranged in descending order of importance. Pope, through the line,

Men, monkeys, lap-dogs, parrots, perish all!

is able to suggest the frivolous mentality and the lack of standards of the fashionable young lady of his day.

Figures of Meaning and Associated Ideas tend to be more powerful in their operation, including as they do simile and metaphor, the foundation figures of speech.

It was Aristotle, the ancient Greek critic, who was of the opinion that the quality of a poet, and hence of poetry, could be established by the originality and fitness of the metaphors and similes employed. It is perhaps not too fanciful to assert that the 'discovery' of metaphor and simile were to civilisation just as important as the discovery of fire or the wheel: or to say that a metaphor or a simile was the first encyclopedia, because in using one, man took the first step towards creating order out of the diversity of objects around him by seeing some identity in two of them.

Let's look at metaphor, while remembering that to deal with metaphor in detail and examine all the ways in which it operates would require a whole book in itself. In metaphor, which can operate using noun, verb, adjective or adverb, we refer to something in terms of something else which, for the metaphor-maker, has some resemblance to it. In fact, metaphor is so prevalent in language that it could be claimed as the way in which language develops rather than a mere 'figure of speech'. When we see something unfamiliar we tend to bring it into our mental cosmos by seeing it in terms of something with which we are familiar. (A new animal becomes 'hippopotamus' a 'river-horse'); or when the poet sees himself or his environment in a new light he may see similarities not normally present. Hence English is full of dead, dying and living metaphors and will be enriched by others yet unborn.

'Dead' metaphors, as they are called, are metaphors that have ceased to be thought of as involving any figurative comparison. We used one a page or two back: 'are brought into play'. They are part of everyday speech. Common are terms of endearment such as sweetie, honey, hen, or ducks, or such as 'the eye of a needle', 'the mouth of a river', or 'the brow (or crest) of a hill', or metaphors of movement such as 'waltzed into the room' or 'shot him an angry look' or 'flew upstairs'. This is what the American writer, Emerson, meant when he said 'Language is fossil poetry'. (What is the point of the metaphor in that statement?)

'Dying' metaphors or 'tired' metaphors are those that have been used so often that they are in process of losing the point of the original identification. They make for boring conversation, bad prose and worse poetry—except where they are used for special effects. You can compile your own list of 'gems' from political oratory or listen to a take-off by Peter Sellers.

To be effective, the metaphors, or similes, of poetry have to be fresh, vivid and original. In a good metaphor the terms of the comparison must not be too close together, the similarity must not be too obvious, but on the other hand the metaphor, or simile, will fail in its object if the distance between the two terms is too great and the similarity between them is too difficult to spot. The good metaphor delights us by being apt in the context in which it occurs, and by making us see relationships we had not seen before but which we recognise as being there when brought before us. When Hopkins began his sonnet *God's Grandeur* with the lines

> The world is charged with the grandeur of God.
> It will flame out, like shining from shook foil;

he saw the power and majesty of God revealing themselves in nature in the same way as a body contains an electric charge. Take phrases such as Sylvia Plath's 'A vulturous boredom' or R. S. Thomas's 'with clenched thoughts', or Peter Redgrove's

> My secret darted into hiding behind the sun's throbbing

or

> The moon was a ghostly galleon tossed upon cloudy seas

On the other hand, we give you some unusual ones without comment. (Argue about them.) Charles Causley has:

> Timothy Winters comes to school
> With eyes as wide as a football-pool
> Ears like bombs and teeth like splinters
> A blitz of a boy is Timothy Winters.

Norman McCaig about frogs:

> that die
> Like Italian tenors.

The anonymous author of *Polly Perkins* on a handsome man:

> His hair must be curly as any watch spring
> And his whiskers as big as a brush for clothing.

Another mercifully anonymous author said

> Ah no, Love, not while your hot kisses burn
> Like a potato riding on the blast.

A poet may still be able to freshen up a cliché if he handles it with some dexterity. Bees have for centuries been symbols of industry: 'as busy as a bee'. Louis Macneice in *The British Museum Reading Room* elaborates the comparison, likening the scholars to the bees within a hive:

> Under the hive-like dome the stooping haunted readers
> Go up and down the alleys, tap the cells of knowledge—
> Honey and wax, the accumulation of years . . .

Other figures of speech that come under the present heading are synecdoche and metonymy.

Broadly speaking, figures of speech can serve two main purposes: they can have a logical or clarifying function or they can enhance the emotive impact, even if the emotion is one of laughter. These two purposes, of course, are not mutually exclusive, and a good metaphor, for instance, may well combine both intentions. Most figures of speech, however, tend to lean towards one side or the other, but you can keep the two functions in mind when you are looking critically at a poem.

IMAGERY

In our assessment of a poem one important element to be scrutinised is the imagery. The term 'imagery' is a difficult one to define and has many different uses. The word itself suggests that it is concerned only with the visual sense, with eyesight or things we can conjure up in the mind's eye; and this was the sense in which the word was used in the past. Nowadays, however, the word is taken to mean 'that part of a literary work which appeals to the senses'. This includes all the senses—sight, hearing, touch, taste and smell, although images of sight usually predominate, followed by images of hearing.

In Keats' *Eve of St. Agnes*, notice how the poet appeals to four different senses in the description of the feast Porphyro prepares for Madeline:

> And still she slept an azure-lidded sleep,
> In blanched linen, smooth, and lavender'd,
> While he from forth the closet brought a heap
> Of candied apple, quince, and plum, and gourd,
> With jellies soother than the creamy curd,
> And lucent syrops, tinct with cinnamon;

and to complete Keats' repertoire with imagery of hearing from the same poem:

> Soon, up aloft,
> The silver, snarling trumpets 'gan to chide.

Modern psychologists now recognise several other senses besides the traditional five illustrated above. They include one of importance for poetry—the *kinaesthetic* sense which relates to our sense of movement or awareness of bodily effort. For instance, in *Thrushes* from the phrase 'and drag out some writhing thing' you get the impression of muscular effort in the use of 'drag out'. Or in Peter Whigham's line, 'then the worm gnaws with a purpose'.

You will probably have noticed that images in poetry frequently occur as the terms in similes and metaphors and at one time the term 'imagery' was restricted to such figurative uses of language. You must now use it to include any concrete appeal to the senses, the literal as well as the figurative. If you look at the *Prelude* by Eliot that begins 'The Winter evening settles down' the only line where language is being used figuratively is 'The burnt out ends of smoky days' and the 'settles down' of the first line. All the other concrete sensuous details of the thirteen lines are used literally to evoke atmosphere and therefore to be regarded as the 'imagery' of the poem.

A group of poets calling themselves the 'imagists' had a considerable influence on poetry at the beginning of the century and that influence has in one form or another continued till today. Strongly influenced by Chinese poetry, they insisted that sharp visual images were the essence of poetry, and some of the extreme maintained that a poem could be constructed of visual images alone, without grammatical statements. Take these lines of Ezra Pound, written under the influence of 'Imagist' theories:

> The apparition of those faces in the crowd;
> Petals on a wet, black bough

or T. E. Hulme, one of the leaders of the imagist movement:

> And saw the ruddy moon lean over a hedge
> Like a red-faced farmer.

Not infrequently you will come across what is rather awesomely called *synaesthetic* imagery which has been mentioned before as a device of language. In this the poet refers to one sense in terms of another sense. It has appeared more and more in poetry as this century has progressed, although earlier, for example, Emily Dickinson referred to a fly's 'blue, uncertain, stumbling buzz'. Rimbaud, a French poet, wrote a sonnet on the colour of vowels. It might be easier for you to try to apply colours to the sounds of some of the musical instruments of an orchestra. We do use synaesthetic imagery in every day life, without noticing it. Everyone knows what we mean by a 'soft' whisper or 'loud' or 'crying' colours or a 'hard' voice.

The importance of imagery is that it can evoke atmosphere, as in Eliot's *Prelude*, or it can suggest meanings without the poet having to make these meanings explicit. As in free verse every line tends to be a movement of its own, of thought, of feeling, of action, of image, it frequently happens that lines consist only of images, often in the form of a minor sentence, i.e. a sentence without a finite verb.

When you read *Hamlet* you will find it full of 'disease' images, particularly of festering diseases like ulcers and abscesses which reinforce Hamlet's belief that 'something is rotten in the state of Denmark'. And in Macbeth's soliloquy 'If it were done when 'tis done', although he says if he could get away with murder on earth, he would 'jump (take a chance on) the life to come', nevertheless images such as 'angels trumpet-tongued', 'deep damnation', 'heaven's cherubim' show that, subconsciously perhaps, he is shown by Shakespeare as affected by the possible consequences in the next life. Notice in Ted Hughes' *Thrushes* the imagery is used to manipulate our responses. In dealing with the instinctive reactions of the birds there are repeated references to metallic, mechanical images, particularly those of energy released explosively—'coiled steel', 'triggered', 'bullet and automatic purpose', 'efficiency' and 'streamlined'—whereas when he comes to deal with the human being the imagery takes on a religious character—'his act worships itself', 'he bends to be blent in prayer', 'distracting devil's orgy' and 'hosannah', suggesting the religious devotion with which man pursues his conscious purposes and the distractions which divert him from them.

In any poem you should examine the imagery, see whether certain kinds of image occur, and try to assess the purpose behind their use.

SYMBOLISM

Sometimes when we read a poem we get a feeling that although the poet is talking of one thing he is really suggesting something else indirectly. Take William Blake's poem, *The Sick Rose*:

> O Rose, thou art sick!
> The Invisible worm,
> That flies in the night,
> In the howling storm,
>
> Has found out thy bed
> Of crimson joy;
> And his dark secret love
> Does thy life destroy.

It is fairly obvious that although on the literal level the poem purports to be about an actual rose and an actual worm, these items can stand for something else. The poet is, in fact, using them as symbols, although just exactly what they stand for is difficult to determine in this case.

Symbolism occurs at different levels of difficulty. Some symbols are easy to grasp, for they have become part of the traditional culture of the race or the civilisation employing them. In our European-American culture there is no problem in understanding such an expression as 'washed in the blood of the Lamb' which, to anyone coming fresh to it from an alien culture would either be taken literally, with horrific conclusions or be regarded as non-sensical (indeed poets often may seem to be writing nonsense until their symbols are properly decoded.) A great number of words have become part of the language stock through folk tradition, religion, history and literature.

There are numerous symbols drawn from nature. A rose is a symbol for beauty, fire for physical passion. You could easily attach their symbolic meaning to the ant, the owl and the serpent. Water (think of baptism) is the symbol of life-giving power, the desert of sterility. The lily is the emblem of death so that Keats can say of the Knight in *La Belle Dame sans Merci* 'I see a lily on thy brow', and we know the hand of death is upon him. Whiteness is traditionally associated with purity and innocence, yellow with jealousy and cowardice, black with evil or sorrow. The moon because of its changing shape and appearance has been used to mean inconstancy. Once, too, though only a few relics remain, there was a language of flowers, as you can see from Ophelia in the 'mad scene' in *Hamlet*. Using natural symbols Milton opens *Lycidas* with

> Yet once more, O ye laurels, and once more
> Ye myrtles brown, with ivy never sere,
> I come to pluck your berries harsh and crude.

We can easily deduce that he means he is undertaking the difficult task of writing a poem that will bring him lasting poetic fame.

None of you would have much trouble in assigning another meaning to Adam, Eve, or Methuselah, or to the Cross, the Shepherd or Calvary, though you might have a little more trouble with a 'Pisgah view' or Ananias or Mammon. In history Scots have no need to be reminded of the symbolic use of Bannockburn and Flodden. In the British coronation ceremony the monarch by long-standing custom is given a crown, an orb, a sword and a sceptre, symbols of certain qualities that pertain to the office of kingship— 'His sceptre shows the force of temporal power'. Thus for some hundreds of years the lines

> Sceptre and Crown
> Must tumble down,
> And in the dust be equal made
> With the poor crookéd scythe and spade

have been immediately clear to the reader. And symbolic figures have come down to us, partly through literature, such as Croesus, Pygmalion, Midas, Oedipus, Cleopatra and Napoleon. If you are alert while reading, you can easily spot when such words are used literally and when symbolically, and can understand the commonly accepted meaning behind their use.

A much more difficult problem arises when a poet invents a symbolism of his own or invests existing symbols with his private meaning. For example, William Blake has a large mass of poetry in which the symbols are so private that it is doubtful if they will ever be so satisfactorily explained as to allow a coherent structure of thought to be seen. In this century two of the greatest poets, Yeats and Eliot, have constructed poetry on the basis of their idiosyncratic symbolism. Many of their poems cannot be fully understood unless we deliberately acquaint ourselves with the symbolic system they employ. When in *Gerontion* Eliot writes

> Rocks, moss, stonecrop, iron, merds

we cannot see the point of the line in the context unless we understand that rocks stand for barrenness, moss and stonecrop for torpor or lassitude, iron for mechanisation and merds for corruption.

This is not to say that their poems cannot still be enjoyed on a more surface level for other qualities.

Let us take two poems to show different levels of difficulty in the use of symbolic language. First Yeats'

> I made my song a coat
> Covered with embroideries
> Out of old mythologies
> From heel to throat;
> But the fools caught it,
> Wore it in the world's eyes
> As though they'd wrought it.
> Song, let them take it,
> For there's more enterprise
> In walking naked.

From the clues in the poem the 'embroideries' represent the decorative imagery from Celtic legend and the myths Yeats used in his earlier poetry. So 'in walking naked' means a new style of poetic writing. Perhaps the figure here is more metaphor than symbol, for these often shade into one another. (Can you detect the ambiguity in the first line?)

In the Yeats poem we can pin down the interpretation to specific words. But symbolism is often subtler, or more difficult to determine. In Robert Frost's *Stopping by the Woods on a Snowy Evening* is sleep to be taken with its literal meaning? Let us look more closely at Stevie Smith's *Not Waving but Drowning*:

> Nobody heard him, the dead man,
> But still he lay moaning:
> I was much further out than you thought
> And not waving but drowning.

Poor chap, he always loved larking
And now he's dead
It must have been too cold for him his heart gave way,
They said

Oh, no no no, it was too cold always
(Still the dead one lay moaning)
I was much too far out all my life
And not waving but drowning.

On the surface this is a drowning tragedy told in contrastive light-hearted language and rhythms. How far ought we to see this story of the man whose signal of distress was misunderstood as having a deeper meaning about the plight of human beings in, and some throughout, life when desperately in need of help? How far is it a commentary on the plight of all men just because they have to live in a world never completely understood, never completely understanding?

You will already have gathered some of the aspects of symbolism. Perhaps it would be advisable for you to consider the following:

1. Symbols may be precise but they may also remain vague and inexact, triggering off your imagination, suggesting significance rather than making clear-cut references.

2. Symbolism, as you will have gathered from the Yeats poem, seems to verge on metaphor, and it is present in other figures of speech, such as metonymy (in some of its forms) and in antonomasia. For example, when Morris in *The Haystack and the Floods* says of one character 'That Judas, Godmar' he is using Judas as a symbol for treacherousness. The power of the figure derives from the aptness with which the symbol fits the human context, how representative the individual is of the general type denoted by the symbol. Generally it acts by a form of magnification, intensification and surprise.

3. Most symbolic words are also in themselves part of the imagery of the poem and can be looked at for the part they play as images, apart from their contribution to the lexical meaning.

4. We accept that, as in metaphor, there is a correspondence between the two terms involved. But whereas in metaphor the correspondence is because of points of similarity, in symbol there is no similarity, except that deliberately constructed by the mind.

5. There is a clear connection between symbol and allegory. Spenser in *The Faerie Queene* made the characters of history symbolic, not only of contemporary historical people, but also of the qualities of human life. Gray in his *Ode on a Favourite Cat*, with which you will be familiar, uses a mixture of symbol and allegory with the cat as the symbol of a girl or girlhood in general.

6. Symbolism can be used with extreme subtlety. In *The Waste Land* Eliot in the passage beginning 'The Chair she sat in' wants us to think of Cleopatra and the qualities she represents in Shakespeare's *Antony and Cleopatra* as a symbolic contrast to the modern aristocrat and the quality of her life.

STRUCTURE OF A POEM

Up till now we have considered the different elements in poetry—the sound system, syntax, imagery and so on. We have isolated them for our purpose in a very arbitrary way, for we must always remember that all the elements are fused together in the printed text and act simultaneously.

Edward Lucie-Smith has said:

> I've gradually come to see how much I'm obsessed by the idea of 'poetic architecture': by which I mean that I think of each poem as being a logical orderly structure, obeying rules which are determined by the 'purpose' of the poem.

We now look at the ways in which the different elements can be organised. We must examine the structure of a poem. By the structure of a poem we don't mean simply the stanza form, metre, and rhythm in a regular poem, or the metrical patterns and line lengths in a free verse poem. We mean the organising principle behind the poem, the way the thought or mood is presented—what has led one contemporary poet to assert that poems organise themselves. It is possible to describe an Italian sonnet as consisting of an octave and a sestet of a particular rhyme scheme, the octave being generally a statement of the theme and the sestet an illustration or development of it. Or a Shakespearean sonnet as consisting of four quatrains of alternating rhyme in which the quatrains present the theme in the form of some kind of problem which is solved in the final couplet. But this merely describes the mechanics of its construction, its form or the general process of its development. What we are after in *structure* is the principle undergirding the total word structure of each specific poem.

How a poet structures any poem will depend, of course, on what he is trying to express and the purpose he has in mind. The simplest structures are probably those of narrative and descriptive poems. In the first instance the structure is provided by the time sequence of events, in the second the details of the description provide the structural basis. Even here, however, some sort of selection and arrangement has to be made by the poet. Notice for example in Wordsworth's *Simon Lee* how the elements of narrative are carefully chosen to lead up the last lines:

> Alas! the gratitude of men
> Hath oftener left me mourning.

In other poems the possible varieties of structure are numberless and we can look at only a few examples to show a method. In passing, however, it is wise to look at all poems, especially modern poems, where the repetition of a line or of syntactical pattern occurs, to see its significance in the poetic structure as in *The Force that through the Green Fuse Drives the Flower*. In modern poetry, too, scrutinise carefully the last line or lines, which often yield a clue as to the elements of the poem. We have already seen in Yeats' *A Coat* how a metaphor/symbol can provide a structural framework for a short poem.

The following sonnet of Shakespeare provides a fine example of a poem in which the organising principle is a dominant metaphor which is developed in its details:

> When to the sessions of sweet silent thought
>   I summon up remembrance of things past,
> I sigh the lack of many a thing I sought,
>   And with old woes new wail my dear time's waste;
>
> Then can I drown an eye, unused to flow,
>   For precious friends hid in death's dateless night,
> And weep afresh love's long-since-cancell'd woe,
>   And moan the expense of many a vanish'd sight.
>
> Then can I grieve at grievances foregone,
>   And heavily from woe to woe tell o'er

The sad account of fore-bemoaned moan,
Which I new pay as if not paid before:

—But if the while I think on thee, dear friend,
All losses are restored, and sorrows end.

The whole sonnet is based on the idea of someone balancing grief and happiness like someone balancing books. Shakespeare seems to have had in mind the ways in which the Exchequer did its annual accounts in Elizabethan days. Hence we have such words as 'sessions', 'summon', 'remembrance' (Government cheques are still drawn on the Queen's 'Remembrancer'), 'time's waste', 'dateless', 'long-since-cancell'd', 'expense', 'foregone', 'tell' (meaning 'count' as in 'Every shepherd tells his tale'), 'account', 'pay' and 'losses'. You can, if you have time, scrutinise the language of master and servant in Shakespeare's sonnet that begins:

Being your slave what should I do but tend

or the imagery of the seasons in

How like a winter hath my absence been.

In Ted Hughes' *Thrushes* the structure is built on a contrast between the animal world and the human world. The first stanza describes the thrushes and their instinctive, automatic movements, the second stanza discusses, partly in irony, partly in revulsion, the intense concentration of purpose, and the final stanza deals with the very different situation of the human beings. Notice, too, how the explicit comparison with man in the final stanza is briefly foreshadowed in the first stanza in the lines 'no indolent procrastinations and no yawning stares/No sighs or head-scratchings'.

John Donne's lyrics frequently take the form of arguments, in which propositions are developed logically to the conclusion the poet wishes. Hence many even of his love poems are wrought through clauses of condition and concession, and with the connectives more usually found in discursive prose, such as 'if', 'although', 'yet', 'therefore', as in these verses from *A Valediction: forbidding mourning*.

Our two soules therefore, which are one,   *therefore*
Though I must goe, endure not yet   *though*
A breach, but in expansion
Like gold to ayery thinnesse beate

> If they be two, they are two so   *If*
>   As stiff twin compasses are two
> Thy soul the first foot, makes no show
>   To move, but doth, if th'other doe   *if*
>
> And though it in the center sit,   *though*
>   Yet when the other far doth rome,   *yet*
> It leaves and hearkens after it,
> And grows erect, as that comes home.

Notice, too, how his rather extravagant concept of the soul as a pair of compasses is nevertheless expressed in very ordinary language.

This logical, argumentative structure is very popular with other seventeenth-century poets. For an example, look at Marvell's *To His Coy Mistress*. The whole structure is firmly based on the premises and conclusion of a logical argument, namely

if (1) then (2) but (3) therefore (4)

(1) Had we but world enough and time
(2) This coyness, lady, were no crime
(3) But always at my back I hear
     Times winged chariot hurrying near.
(4) Now, therefore, . . . let us sport us while we may.

These are only a few examples to show how poets structure their work. Obviously you cannot learn from them what is done in any other poem, for every poem is a unique printed product and must be treated as such.

We have now dealt with the main elements you ought to be aware of when you approach a poem for the purposes of Practical Criticism or, indeed, to gain the greatest pleasure from reading it. They can be thought of broadly as *matter* and *manner*. This is what the French poet Mallarmé meant when he chided his friend, the painter Degas, who amused himself by writing sonnets. Degas found, as you may have found so far in writing poetry, that he had a blockage, that he could no longer produce his sonnets. He complained to Mallarmé that his poems would not come out, although he had excellent ideas. Mallarmé's reply was 'Poetry is not written with ideas, but with words'.

Now try to apply to the following short extracts the information you have had in this chapter on the various aspects of meaning.

You can also, of course, make use of what you have learned about the sound and grammatical elements.

Exercises—Meaning

1. Don't be sucked in by the su-superior,
   don't swallow the culture bait,
   don't drink, don't drink, don't get beerier and beerier,
   do learn to discriminate.

   D. H. Lawrence: *Don'ts*

2. Overnight, very
   Whitely, discreetly,
   Very quietly

   Our toes, our noses
   Take hold on the loam,
   Acquire the air.

   Sylvia Plath: *Mushrooms*

3. The slow muffle of hours. Clouds grow visible
   Altering course the morn congeals on a new
   Bearing. Northwards again, and Europe recedes
   With the first sharp splinters of dawn.

   Alan Ross: *Night Patrol*

4. September has flung a spray of rooks
      On the sea-chart of the sky,
   The tall shipmasts crack in the forest
      And the banners of autumn fly.

   Charles Causley: *The Seasons in Cornwall*

5. The sea is a hungry dog,
   Gaunt and grey.
   He rolls on the beach all day,
   With his clashing teeth and shaggy jaws
   Hour upon hour he gnaws
   The rumbling, tumbling stones,

   James Reeves: *The Sea*

6. (The poet has put into a dust-bin a bird he has killed)

    When I emptied the tea-leaves
    This morning I saw
    The bird I killed
    Leaning its head
    On a broken egg-shell.

    George MacBeth: The Bird

7. Swallowing earth through his nose
    The worm inches his miles;
    The fine grain at the grassroots stirs
    And his limy lips nibble in day—

    Peter Redgrove: A Leaf from My Bestiary

8. Summer hangs drugged from sky to earth
    In limpid fathoms of silence:
    Only warm dark dimples of sound
    Slide like slow bubbles
    From the contented throats.

    Richard Kell: Pigeons

9. Beautiful Loch Leven, near by Kinross,
    For a good day's fishing the angler is seldom at a loss,
    For the loch it abounds with pike and trout,
    Which can be had for the catching without any doubt;
    And the scenery around it is most beautiful to be seen,
    Especially the Castle, wherein was imprisoned Scotland's
        ill-starred Queen.

    Wm. McGonagall: Loch Leven

10. Ten speechless knuckles lie along a knee
    Among their veins, gone crooked over voyages
    Made by this ancient captain.

    Lawrence Durrell: A Rhodian Captain

11. I see him old, trapped in a burly house
    Cold in the angry spitting of a rain
    Come down these sixty years.

    George Barker: A Pauper

12. I sweep. One gyrates like a top and falls
     And stunned, stone blind, and deaf
     Buzzes its frightful F
     And dies between three cannibals.

Karl Shapiro: *The Fly*

13. The darkness drops again; but now I know
     That twenty centuries of stony sleep
     Were vexed to nightmare by a rocking cradle,
     And what rough beast, its hour come round at last,
     Slouches towards Bethlehem to be born?

W. B. Yeats: *The Second Coming*

14. Upon the ecstatic diving board the diver,
     poised for parabolas, lets go
     lets go his manshape to become a bird,
     Is bird, and topsy-turvy
     the pool floats overhead, and the white tiles snow
     their crazy hexagons. Is dolphin. Then
     is plant with lilies bursting from his heels.

A. M. Klein: *Lone Bather*

15. And even as this little orb in splendor,
     When will the glory of man's mind, elate,
     Also launch up his heart above the murky,
     The thick and earthly atmosphere of hate?

Louis Ginsberg: *Man-Made Satellite*

Cautionary Thought

Now that you have got this length, and, we hope, have had at least some enjoyment from the getting here, and before you go on to the exercises, we would ask you not to imagine that you have more than dipped a toe into the waters of Practical Criticism. We invite you to look at an expert at work on two lines of text, Professor Geoffrey Tillotson in his edition of *The Rape of the Lock* in the Methuen's

English Classics series. He examines, among others, this couplet from the poem:

> Or stain her Honour, or her new Brocade,
> Forget her Prayers, or miss a Masquerade.

'In that couplet we can separate out the following strips:

(*a*) "Or stain her Honour"
(*b*) "or her new Brocade"
(*c*) "Forget her Prayers"
(*d*) "or miss a Masquerade"

We may say, first of all, that (a) + (b) is parallel to (c) + (d). We may also say that (a) is parallel to (b), and (c) to (d). But we note that, while (a) + (b) is parallel to (c) + (d) on two counts, first as sound and general construction, and second as meaning, (a) is parallel to (b) as sound and (c) to (d) but (a) is contrary to (b) as meaning and (c) to (d). If we read these lines carelessly, mainly for sound. . . . we see that carelessness has tricked us! The sound, the syntax, says one thing, the meaning another and, our carelessness shaken off, the similarity in the sound acts as a catapult projecting us full against the satiric meaning. The sound says: "Young ladies think these things, (a) and (b), (c) and (d), are the same things: they distinguish no difference in value". The meaning says: "No things could be more different than (a) and (b), (c) and (d). And when sound and meaning unite their voices, they say "These things are different, though young ladies slur over the differences". Pope's meaning is often achieved through his metre as much as his words.'

PART TWO

A Method of Attack

In Part 1 of this book, in our search for the total significance of a poem, we dealt with the various contributory elements one by one. We began with the simplest, the sound element, and ended with the most complex, the element of meaning. You should have provided yourselves with a tool kit for dealing with the language resources of the poet.

Of course, you don't approach any poem by looking piecemeal at its various elements in the order we have adopted, nor in isolation from each other. How then do you tackle a poem for Practical Criticism; for giving it the serious attention in reading that the poet has given in the writing of it? We suggest a method:

1. Because of the nature of language itself you must inevitably in your first reading, or readings, concentrate on getting the meaning clear. You must try to establish for yourselves the theme of the poem, the kind of experience the poet is dealing with, and the sequence of thoughts or images by which these are communicated to you. After all, the other elements of language are there only to clarify, intensify or highlight what the poet has to say. This does not mean that you will not be aware of other aspects as you read for the meaning: indeed, you ought to notice every little flick of appreciation or disappointment in your response. Watching your own reactions is part of the basis of good criticism, so long as you can pinpoint the reasons for each response. But, once you have established meaning, you must remember that your further searches may reveal still more meaning than you had originally settled for on first readings, or may cause you to modify what you first decided on.

2. Once you have your idea of theme and thought you should try to say the poem to yourselves with the kind of rhythms and emphases and pauses intended by the poet. Try to say it in *his* way not in your own. Through this you are likely to become aware of at least some of the sources of power, such as the use of sound, and the kinds of grammatical structures, utilised in the poem's making.

3. You are then in a position to make a detailed analysis of the devices used, the purposes for which they are used, what they

contribute to the total significance, and how well they realise the poet's purpose; everything that gives the thought its particular power. Of course, poets vary, poems vary, in the amounts and the kinds of technical resources used. It is your business to observe and be able to comment appropriately on what you find distinctive.

4. You may then, finally, come to some opinion about what the poet means you to understand about, or learn from, the experience he has sought to communicate—his page from his 'reading of life'.

To lead you gradually towards the desired state in which you can tackle a poem on its own and write a worthwhile critical appreciation of it, we have graded the exercises.

In group A we have provided, for each poem, a large number of questions designed to direct your attention to specific aspects of the poem's significance. Normally these will require only brief answers, though you should make as many valid points in each answer as you can.

In group B we have reduced the number of the questions, and thus the amount of direction given to you so that you will need to do more exploration on your own. Your answers will therefore need to be rather more expansive.

In group C we have left the number of questions to a minimum. Your answers to such questions may involve you in a scrutiny of a number of details of various kinds, and they should be fairly lengthy.

In group D we merely give you a number of poems of which you have to give a critical appreciation without any guidance other than yourself and your acquired expertise.

As preparation for the ultimate aim of group D, it is open to you, for any poem, once you have answered the questions, to write a critical appreciation. For group D, and for any of the other poems you want to treat in this way, we suggest that you may find some advantage in the following plan:

(a) The area of life dealt with.
(b) The poet's attitude or attitudes displayed.
(c) The various language resources deployed and how effective they are.
(d) The success of the poem in what it seems to you it sets out to do.
(e) Its value as a comment on, a statement about, a revelation of, an aspect of living.

What passing-bells for these who die as cattle?
Only the monstrous anger of the guns.
Only the stuttering rifles' rapid rattle
Can patter out their hasty orisons.
5   No mockeries for them from prayers or bells,
        Nor any voice of mourning save the choirs,—
The shrill, demented choirs of wailing shells;
        And bugles calling for them from sad shires.
What candles may be held to speed them all?
10   Not in the hands of boys, but in their eyes
Shall shine the holy glimmers of good-byes.
    The pallor of girls' brows shall be their pall;
Their flowers the tenderness of silent minds,
And each slow dusk a drawing-down of blinds.

WILFRED OWEN

1. What is the image that is the basis of the structure of the poem?
2. What part is played in the structuring by the questions of line 1 and line 9?
3. What contrast does the poet effect by 'passing-bells' and 'die as cattle' in line 1?
4. How does he unite the ideas of 'passing-bells' and 'die' in line 8?
5. What is the effect of the lack of finite verbs in the first eight lines?
6. 'Candles' in line 9 introduces the idea of light. Trace the developments of light in the remaining lines.
7. Comment on the effect of the parallelism in lines 3 and 4.
8. Contrast the use made of 'choirs' in line 6 and line 7.
9. Compare the use of sound in lines 2 and 3 with the use in lines 13 and 14.
10. Comment on:
    (*a*) monstrous, line 2.
    (*b*) mockeries, line 5.
    (*c*) Their flowers, line 13.

'There is not much that I can do,
For I've no money that's quite my own!'
Spoke up the pitying child—
A little boy with a violin
5   At the station before the train came in,—
'But I can play my fiddle to you
And a nice one 'tis, and in good tone!'

The man in the handcuffs smiled;
The constable looked, and he smiled, too,
10   As the fiddle began to twang;
And the man in the handcuffs suddenly sang
        With grimful glee:
        'This life so free
        Is the thing for me!'
15   And the constable smiled, and said no word,
As if unconscious of what he heard;
And so they went on till the train came in—
The convict, and the boy with the violin.

THOMAS HARDY

1. The poem concerns three people. What is the attitude of each to the situation?
2. Suggest why the poet uses 'child', 'man in the handcuffs' and 'constable', giving them no names.
3. Why did the constable and the man in the handcuffs smile?
4. Bring out the irony of lines 14 and 15.
5. What is achieved by a short first verse as compared with a longer second verse?
6. Comment on the irregularity of the rhyme scheme in verse 1 as compared with the rhyme scheme in verse 2.
7. What rhyme links the first verse to the second? Comment.
8. How does 'twang' in line 10 contrast with the boy's earlier claim? And why is 'twang' appropriate to the situation?
9. Comment on:

    (*a*) suddenly, line 11.
    (*b*) till the train came in, line 17.

Growing used to a town
I learn the faces:
In the same shop door
The child is always playing
5   Who will never grow up.

Growing used to a town
I go away and return;
And always it surprises me
How many children
10   With dirty graces,
Their stockings twisted like plaits
And their plaits coming undone,
Have changed into slender self-conscious girls
And how many children remain.

MICHAEL BALDWIN

1. What does the poet find surprising about a town?
2. The opening line of both verses is the same. Why?
3. The second lines of each verse are different. In what way do they prepare for what comes after them?
4. In verse 1 the poet uses 'child', 'door' in the singular. The nouns in the second verse are mostly plural. What is the point brought out by the singular in verse 1 and the plurals in verse 2?
5. Bring out the full significance of the figure of speech contained in the last two lines of verse 1.
6. How does the unusual combination of words 'dirty graces' prepare for what follows?
7. What is the significance of 'coming undone' in line 12?
8. Contrast the images before and after 'like plaits'. What function has the simile in the structure of the poem?
9. What does the poet get by having the grammatical structure ASPC in line 8?
10. Bring out the full meaning of 'And how many children remain'.
11. How does the poet get, by the sound of the words he chooses, the effect of untidiness in line 11? Contrast it with the sounds, rhythm and length of line 13.

I sit in the dusk. I am all alone.
Enter a child and an ice-cream cone.

A parent is easily beguiled
By sight of this coniferous child.

5   The friendly embers warmer gleam,
The cone begins to drip ice-cream.

Cones are composed of many a vitamin
My lap is not the place to bitamin.

Although my raiment is not chinchilla,
10   I flinch to see it become vanilla.

Coniferous child, when vanilla melts
I'd rather it melted somewhere else.

Exit child with remains of cone.
I sit in the dusk. I am all alone,

15   Muttering spells like an angry Druid,
Alone, in the dusk, with the cleaning fluid.

OGDEN NASH

1. How does the poet set his scene and introduce his characters?
2. How does he heighten the comedy by the introduction of the seemingly irrelevant?
3. How well does 'Tableau' in the title suit the poet's method of presentation?
4. Compare the first and seventh verses and show what the poet does, and what he achieves by it.
5. Consider the first and second lines of verses 3 and 4. In each case how is the comic effect obtained?
6. Account for the comedy of the last two lines from the structure of the poem.
7. What is the effect of the unusual rhymes where they occur?
8. Say what you can, considering lexical and sound elements, about the rhyme of the last verse.
9. What view of himself does the poet induce us to take?
10. Does the poet make a valid comment about the parent-child relationship?
11. Comment on:

    (*a*) coniferous, line 4.   (*c*) I'd rather, line 12.
    (*b*) lap, line 8.   (*d*) spells, line 15.

Drink to me only with thine eyes,
   And I will pledge with mine;
Or leave a kiss but in the cup
   And I'll not ask for wine.
5   The thirst that from the soul doth rise
   Doth ask a drink divine;
But might I of Jove's nectar sup,
   I would not change for thine.

I sent thee late a rosy wreath,
10   Not so much honouring thee
As giving it the hope that there
   It could not wither'd be;
But thou thereon didst only breathe
   And sent'st it back to me;
15   Since when it grows, and smells, I swear,
   Not of itself but thee!

B. JONSON

Note: This poem was written in the early 1600's. Ben Jonson, with his cronies of the *Mermaid Tavern*, was a noted convivial drinker. In the ritual of social drinking of the time, *to drink to someone* was to pay them a compliment or wish them success, health, etc. (see the same idea in Burns *Gae fetch to me a pint of wine*). For a lady to compliment a company of gentlemen and be automatically complimented, she would take a sip from a wine cup from which the gentlemen would then drink. She was held then to be kissing them by remote control (see the same idea in Goldsmith's *The Deserted Village*: 'kiss the cup, to pass it to the rest').

1. In verse 1 what are the various ways in which the poet compliments the lady?
2. What position towards her does the poet assume. Support your statement by quotation.
3. In verse 1, line 5 suddenly widens the perspective. How?
4. How much of literal truth and how much of fantasy is there in verse 2?
5. In what way is the fantasy a development from the last three lines of verse 1?

6. What permanent truth about people in love is behind the idea of the last two lines? Justify your choice.
7. Which image do you think to contain the best compliment paid to the lady?
8. Are you disturbed by the use of archaic words in the poem? Give your reactions and try to justify your point of view.
9. Notice the very formal pattern into which he arranges his ideas. Is he a pretty cold, intellectual lover because of it?
10. What change of meaning is there between 'ask' in line 4 and 'ask' in line 6?
11. What part does the rhyme scheme play in knitting all the ideas of a verse together?
12. Notice those lines where the poet in both verses places the stress on the initial word of the line. What effect has this at those points?

They dunno how it is. I smack a ball
right through the goals. But they dunno how the words
get muddled in my head, get tired somehow.
I look through the window, see. And there's a wall
5   I'd kick the ball against, just smack and smack.
Old Jerry, he can't play, he don't know how,
not now at any rate. He's too flicking small.
See him in shorts, out in the crazy black.
Rythm, he says, and ryme. See him at back.
10 He don't know nothing about Law. He'd fall
flat on his face, just like a big sack,
when you're going down the wing, the wind behind you
And crossing into the goalmouth and they're roaring
the whole great crowd. They're on their feet cheering.
15 The ball's at your feet and there it goes, just crack.
Old Jerry dives—the wrong way. And they're jeering
and I run to the centre and old Bash
jumps up and down, and I feel great, and wearing
my gold and purpel strip, fresh from the wash.

IAN   CRICHTON   SMITH

1. What are the attractions of football to the speaker of this monologue?
2. What is gained by using direct speech?
3. What two aspects of the boy are brought out in lines 1–3?
4. Who is Old Jerry and who is Law?
5. What is his attidude towards Old Jerry and why has he this attitude?
6. How well by the language chosen does the poet convey that it is a boy who is speaking?
7. How do the grammatical structures bring out the kind of boy he is?
8. What feelings of the boy are conveyed by the structure of the last sentence?
9. Do you think the poet is making a comment about education or about life? If so, what?
10. What indication of the mental ability of the boy is suggested by the kinds of rhyme and the arrangement of the rhymes?

These, in the day when heaven was falling,
The hour when earth's foundations fled,
Followed their mercenary calling
And took their wages and are dead.

5   Their shoulders held the sky suspended;
They stood, and earth's foundations stay;
What God abandoned, these defended,
And saved the sum of things for pay.

A. E. HOUSMAN

1. How does the last line contain all the elements the poet has used previously?
2. Comment on the opening word 'These'.
3. What is the poet's attitude to 'These' in the first verse?
4. How does the attitude change in the second verse, whatever you made of the first verse?
5. What contrasts in idea are there between lines 1 and 2, and lines 3 and 4 of the first verse?
6. How does the grammatical structure in lines 3 and 4 reinforce the ideas expressed?
7. Describe the similarities and contrasts of the first two lines of verse 1 as against the first two lines of verse 2.
8. Why do you think he has repeated 'earth's foundations'?
9. Bring out the force of 'What God abandoned', and the almost blasphemous reinforcement by the figure of speech employed in the whole line.
10. Compare, as lexical items, the verbs in the first verse with the verbs in the second verse.
11. Comment on the effect of the constant use of 'they', 'their', 'these.'
12. There is only one adjective, 'mercenary', in line 4. Comment.

'I shall be careful to say nothing at all
About myself or what I know of him
Or the vaguest thought I have—no matter how dim,
Tonight if it so happen that he call.'

5   And not ten minutes later the doorbell rang
And into the hall he stepped as he always did
With a face and a bearing that quite poorly hid
His brain that burned and his heart that fairly sang
And his tongue that wanted to be rid of the truth.

10   As well as she could, for she was very loath
To signify how she felt, she kept very still,
But soon her heart cracked loud as a coffee mill
And her brain swung like a comet in the dark
And her tongue raced like a squirrel in the park.

MERRILL MOORE

1. What is the mood of the girl in the first verse?
2. How does the poet suggest in the second verse that she will come under heavy pressure?
3. How does the third verse link, in idea, with both of the other verses?
4. What is the point of putting the first verse in direct speech and the other two in indirect speech?
5. What is effected by the half-rhymes of 'truth' and 'loath' in the positions in which they are placed?
6. What attitude is revealed by the grammatical structure of line 4?
7. Comment on the purpose of the similes in lines 12, 13, 14.
8. Examine lines 12, 13 and 14 for words that are repetitions of words in lines 8 and 9. Comment.
9. Twice the poet opens two consecutive lines with 'And'. Compare and contrast her use.

An Old Man

Look at him there on the wet road,
Muffled with smoke, an old man trying
Time's treacherous ice with a slow foot.
Tears on his cheek are the last glitter
5   On bare branches of the long storm
That shook him once leaving him bowed
And destitute as a tree stripped
Of foliage under a bald sky.

Come, then, winter, build with your cold
10   Hands a bridge over those depths
His mind balks at; let him go on,
Confident still; let the hard hammer
Of pain fall with as light a blow
On the brow's anvil as the sun does now.

R. S. THOMAS

1. What is the effect of the imperative of the verb as an opening word?
2. What is the effect of ending the second line with 'trying'?
3. Why does the poet say 'Time's *treacherous* ice' and what words does he also use in lines 2 and 3 to suggest his insecurity and hence our pity?
4. The poet uses the image of a tree in verse one. How does the imagery develop the sense of the man's insecurity and the reader's pity?
5. 'A bald sky'. Bring out the force of 'bald'.
6. What linguistic parallel is there between the opening words of each verse?
7. How does the poet shift our viewpoint in the opening of the second verse?
8. In verse 2 the image is of winter. In what way is winter an easy transition from the tree imagery?
9. In what two senses are we to think of winter in verse 2?
10. What do you think 'the long storm' was?
11. There is only one rhyme, and that is an imperfect rhyme. Why rhyme, and what is the purpose behind the imperfect rhyme?

You may talk o' gin and beer
When you're quartered safe out 'ere,
An' you're sent to penny-fights an' Aldershot it;
But when it comes to slaughter
5   You will do your work on water,
An' you'll lick the bloomin' boots of 'im that's got it.
Now in Injia's sunny clime,
Where I used to spend my time,
A-servin' of 'Er Majesty the Queen,
10   Of all them blackfaced crew
The finest man I knew
Was our regimental bhisti, Gunga Din,

       He was 'Din! Din! Din!
'You limpin' lump o' brick-dust, Gunga Din!
15   'Hi! Slippy *hitherao*!
       'Water, get it! *Panee lao*,
'You squidgy-nosed old idol, Gunga Din.'

RUDYARD KIPLING

1. What persona does the poet adopt?
2. To whom is he talking in his adopted role?
3. What is his attitude towards them?
4. Look at lines 1–3, then lines 4–6. What contrasts are made?
5. Contrast the attitude in lines 11 and 12 with the attitudes expressed through lines 13–17. Can you reconcile them in any way?
6. What effects are obtained by the grammatical structure of lines 10–13?
7. What is the effect of the double rhyme where it is used?
8. Comment on the grammatical structures of lines 13–17.
9. Comment on:
    (*a*) do your work, line 5.
    (*b*) spend my time, line 8.
    (*c*) A-servin' of 'Er Majesty the Queen, line 9.
    (*d*) bhisti, *hitherao*, *Panee lao*, lines 12, 15, 16.

I sat all morning in the College sick bay;
Counting bells knelling classes to a close.
At two o'clock our neighbours drove me home.

In the porch I met my father crying—
5   He had always taken funerals in his stride—
And Big Jim Evans saying it was a hard blow.

The baby cooed and laughed and rocked the pram
When I came in, and I was embarrassed
By old men standing up to shake my hand

10   And tell me they were 'Sorry for my trouble'.
At ten o'clock an ambulance arrived
With the corpse, starched and bandaged by nurses.

Next morning I went up into the room. Snowdrops
And candles soothed the bedside; I saw him
15   For the first time in six weeks. Paler now,

Wearing a puffy bruise on his left temple,
He lay in the four-foot box as in a cot
No gaudy scars, the bumper knocked him clear.

A four-foot box, a foot for every year.

SEAMUS HEANEY

1. This poem has three separate scenes. What are they?
2. Comment on the choice of these scenes and the order in which they
   are arranged.
3. What do you make of the members of the family the poet chooses to
   use?
4. The poet unites life and death in lines 15–18. How? Among other
   things pay attention to 'now', 'wearing', 'bruise' and 'cot'.
5. Comment on the sound and rhythm of line 2.
6. What is the effect of the parenthesis, line 5?

7. Is there any symbolism in the title of the poem?
8. Give your opinion of the last line as an ending to the poem.
9. Comment on:

   (*a*) knelling, line 2.
   (*b*) "sorry for my trouble", line 10

When getting my nose in a book
Cured most things short of school,
It was worth ruining my eyes
To know I could still keep cool,
5   And deal out the old right hook
To dirty dogs twice my size.

Later, with inch-thick specs,
Evil was just my lark:
Me and my cloak and fangs
10   Had ripping times in the dark.
The women I clubbed with sex!
I broke them up like meringues.

Don't read much now: the dude
Who lets the girl down before
15   The hero arrives, the chap
Who's yellow and keeps the store,
Seem far too familiar. Get stewed:
Books are a load of crap.

PHILIP LARKIN

1. Bring out in detail the force of 'Don't read much now' in the structure of the poem.
2. Discuss the imagery used in verses 1 and 2, and the point it makes.
3. In the language used is there a continuous progression of vulgarity?
4. What is the effect of the sentence structure and punctuation in line 11?
5. Get as much as you can out of the last line of the poem.
6. Comment on:

         (*a*) old, line 5.
         (*b*) Me, line 9.
         (*c*) ripping, line 10.
         (*d*) meringues, line 12.

He met her
at the Green Horse
by the Surrey Docks;
Saturday
5   was the colour of his socks.

So they loved,
but loving
made nothing better—
drowning cats
10   in an ocean of water.

What more,
what more could there be,
days or nights?
Nothing
15   to hear or see but dances and sights.

So they loved,
like the aimless air
or like walking
past shut doors
20   in a never quiet street and talking.

PETER LEVI, S.J.

1. 'Aimless'. How well does this suggest the relationship of the two people?
2. The first three lines of each verse have a somewhat similar structure. From them, consider the development of the poet's attitude.
3. In verses 1–3 what is the relationship of the last two lines to the first three lines of each verse?
4. How is the last verse different in structure from the first three verses and what did the poet intend to achieve by it?
5. What do you make of lines 4 and 5?
6. Bring out the significance of the imagery in the last three lines.

The lanky hank of a she in the inn over there,
Nearly killed me for asking the loan of a glass of beer;
May the devil grip the whey-faced slut by the hair,
And beat bad manners out of her skin for a year.

5   That parboiled imp, with the toughest jaw you will see
On virtue's path, and a voice that would rasp the dead,
Came roaring and raging the minute she looked at me,
And threw me out of the house on the back of my head!

If I asked her master he'd give me a cask a day;
10   But she, with the beer at hand, not a gill would arrange!
May she marry a ghost and bear him a kitten, and may
The High King of Glory permit her to get the mange.

JAMES STEPHENS

1. Contrast the situation that gave rise to the poem with the reactions of the speaker.
2. How does the speaker bring out his attitude of injured innocence?
3. Compare the structuring of ideas in the first and third verses.
4. Choose three examples of extravagant language and tell what they contribute to the humour of the poem.
5. Comment on:
   (*a*) loan, line 2.
   (*b*) line 9.
   (*c*) High King of Glory.
   (*d*) the sound and rhythm of the poem.

I met a traveller from an antique land
  Who said: Two vast and trunkless legs of stone
Stand in the desert. Near them on the sand,
  Half sunk, a shatter'd visage lies, whose frown

5   And wrinkled lip and sneer of cold command
  Tell that its sculptor well those passions read
Which yet survive, stamp'd on these lifeless things,
  The hand that mock'd them and the heart that fed;

And on the pedestal these words appear:
10 'My name is Ozymandias, king of kings:
  Look on my works, ye Mighty, and despair!'

Nothing beside remains. Round the decay
  Of that colossal wreck, boundless and bare,
The lone and level sands stretch far away.

P. B. SHELLEY

1. What impression of Ozymandias, past and present, does the poet create in lines 1–11?
2. How do lines 12–14 bring out the irony of the inscription of the pedestal?
3. Concentrating on the language used, discuss the poet's technique in gradually showing Ozymandias as a human being.
4. Compare and contrast the tone and effect of lines 1 and 14.
5. How is sense reinforced by sound in line 14?
6. In terms of stress and rhythm what effect does the poet get from:
     (*a*) Stand in the desert, line 3.
     (*b*) Look on my works, line 11.
     (*c*) Nothing beside remains, line 12.

That one small boy with a face like pallid cheese
And burnt-out little eyes could make a blaze
As brazen, fierce and huge, as red and gold
And zany yellow as the one that spoiled
5   Three thousand guineas' worth of property
And crops at Godwin's Farm on Saturday
Is frightening, as fact and metaphor:
An ordinary match intended for
The lighting of a pipe or kitchen fire
10   Misused may set a whole menagerie
Of flame-fanged tigers roaring hungrily.
And frightening, too, that one small boy should set
The sky on fire and choke the stars to heat
Such skinny limbs and such a little heart
15   Which would have been content with one warm
     kiss,
Had there been anyone to offer this.

VERNON SCANNELL

1. Reveal the two aspects of the boy presented to us by the poet.
2. In the first six lines the poet manipulates similarities and contrasts.
   Show what they are and how he manipulates them.
3. By what devices does the poet modify our attitude to the boy in
   lines 8–16?
4. Look closely at and comment on the rhymes used.
5. Comment on the sentence structure of lines 1–7.
6. What judgement on life does the poet intend to make?
7. Comment on:

   (a) the repetition of 'frightening' in lines 7 and 12.
   (b) menagerie, line 10.

Elvis Presley

Two minutes long it pitches through some bar:
Unreeling from a corner box, the sigh
Of this one, in his gangling finery
And crawling sideburns, wielding a guitar.

5   The limitations where he found success
Are ground on which he, panting, stretches out
In turn, promiscuously, by every note.
Our idiosyncrasy and our likeness.

We keep ourselves in touch with a mere dime:
10   Distorting hackneyed words in hackneyed songs
He turns revolt into a style, prolongs
The impulse to a habit of the time.

Whether he poses or is real, no cat
Bothers to say: the pose held is a stance,
15   Which, generation of the very chance
It wars on, may be posture for combat.

THOM GUNN

1. What impression of the music is given in verses 1 and 2?
2. In verse 2 what comment is made on the singer's style of presentation?
3. What does the poet see the music as a symbol of?
4. In verse 4 what danger does the poet see in such music, and why?
5. Comment on the grammatical structure of line 1 as an opening line.
6. Comment on:

     (a) wielding, line 4.
     (b) mere, line 9.
     (c) generation, line 15.

I have a picture I took in Bombay
of a beggar asleep on the pavement:
grey-haired, wearing shorts and a dirty shirt,
his shadow thrown aside like a blanket.

5   His arms and legs could be cracks in the stone,
routes for the ants' journeys, the flies' descents.
Brain-washed by the sun into exhaustion,
he lies veined into stone, a fossil man.

Behind him there is a crowd passingly
10   bemused by a pavement trickster and quite
indifferent to this very common sight
of an old man asleep on the pavement.

I thought it then a good composition
and glibly called it 'The Man in the Street,'
15   remarking how typical it was of
India that the man in the street lived there.

His head in the posture of one weeping
into a pillow chides me now for my
presumption at attempting to compose
20   art out of his hunger and solitude.

ZULFIKAR GHOSE

1. How do the ideas of the poem justify the ambiguity of the title?
2. Talk about the language the poet uses to dehumanise the beggar at
   the beginning of the poem and re-humanise him at the end.
3. Contrast the tone of verse 4 with the tone of verse 5.
4. Comment on the effect of the line arrangement in verse 3.

I like to see it lap the Miles—
And lick the Valleys up—
And stop to feed itself at Tanks—
And then—prodigious step

5   Around a Pile of Mountains—
And supercilious peer
In Shanties—by the sides of Roads—
And then a Quarry pare

To fit its Ribs
10   And crawl between
Complaining all the while
In horrid—hooting stanza—
Then chase itself down Hill—

And neigh like Boanerges—
15   Then—punctual as a Star
Stop—docile and omnipotent
At its own stable door—

EMILY DICKINSON

1. Deal with the image that is used to structure the poem.
2. Show how the poet has mixed feelings about the train.
3. The whole poem consists of one unfinished sentence. Why?
4. Discuss the various effects gained by the dash and by the lack of any other punctuation.
5. Comment on the rhymes and their employment.
6. How do the rhythms of the last verse contrast with the rhythms in the previous verses. And why?
7. Decide on the intonation and rhythm you would give to the last line. Justify your decision.

Juan, a bachelor, has arrived in England with a young orphan girl,
Leila, whose upbringing is a matter of concern.

    So first there was a general emulation,
       And then there was a general competition,
    To undertake the orphan's education.
       As Juan was a person of condition,
5   It had been an affront on this occasion
       To talk of a subscription or petition;
    But sixteen dowagers, ten unwed she sages,
    Whose tale belongs to 'Hallam's Middle Ages',

    And one or two sad, separate wives, without
10   A fruit to bloom upon their withering bough—
    Begg'd to bring *up* the little girl, and *'out'*,—
       For that's the phrase that settles all things now,
    Meaning a virgin's first blush at a rout,
       And all her points as thorough-bred to show:
15   And I assure you, that like virgin honey
    Tastes their first season (mostly if they have money).

    How all the needy honourable misters,
       Each out-at-elbow peer, or desperate dandy,
    The watchful mothers, and the careful sisters,
20   (Who, by the by, when clever, are more handy
       At making matches, where ''t is gold that glisters',
    Than their *he* relatives), like flies o'er candy
    Buzz round *'the* Fortune' with their busy battery,
    To turn her head with waltzing and with flattery!

25   Each aunt, each cousin, hath her speculation;
       Nay, married dames will now and then discover
    Such pure disinterestedness of passion,
       I've known them court an heiress for their lover.
    'Tantaene!' Such the virtues of high station,
30   Even in the hopeful Isle, whose outlet's 'Dover!'
    While the poor wretch, object of these cares,
    Has cause to wish her sire had had male heirs.

Some are soon bagg'd, and some reject three dozen.

BYRON

1. What picture of English high society does the poet present?
2. Is the poet more cruel than comic in his treatment of people?
3. Consider the imagery of line 14.
4. Show, from the language, how the poet's attitude is that of a well-bred equal of those he is satirising.
5. Discuss the final lines of the third and fourth verses as the end lines of a satirical verse.
6. Does he have sympathy with anyone? Quote to support your view.
7. Comment on the grammatical structure of lines 15, 16.
8. Comment on:

    (*a*) the use of parenthesis.
    (*b*) the use of rhyme.
    (*c*) virtues, line 28.
    (*d*) bagg'd, line 33.

I

In a shoe box stuffed in an old nylon stocking
Sleeps the baby mouse I found in the meadow,
Where he trembled and shook beneath a stick
Till I caught him up by the tail and brought him in,
5   Cradled in my hand,
A little quaker, the whole body of him trembling,
His absurd whiskers sticking out like a cartoon-mouse,
His feet like small leaves,
Little lizard-feet,
10   Whitish and spread wide when he tried to struggle away,
Wriggling like a miniscule puppy.

Now he's eaten his three kinds of cheese and drunk from his
    bottle-cap watering-trough—
So much he just lies in one corner,
His tail curled under him, his belly big
15   As his head; his bat-like ears
Twitching, tilting toward the least sound.

Do I imagine he no longer trembles
When I come close to him?
He seems no longer to tremble.

II

20   But this morning the shoe-box house on the back porch is
    empty.
Where has he gone, my meadow mouse,
My thumb of a child that nuzzled in my palm?—
To run under the hawk's wing,
Under the eye of the great owl watching from the elm-tree,
25   To live by courtesy of the shrike, the snake, the tom-cat.

I think of the nestling fallen into the deep grass,
The turtle gasping in the dusty rubble of the highway,
The paralytic stunned in the tub, and the water rising,—
All things innocent, hapless, forsaken.

THEODORE ROETHKE

1. What impression of the mouse is created in the first section and how does the poet create it?
2. Relate this to the attitude adopted by the poet in the second section.
3. What does the poet mean us to understand about life?
4. Choose three lines, together or separate, from this free verse structure that you feel particularly notable. Justify your choice.

I saw her on the pavement's edge,
Not timid, half-smiling at the crowd
That tumbled round; she did not budge;
Only her eyes moved.

5   A dusky little muzzle like some pretty
Small animal crept from a sun-spotted
Thicket by mistake to this grey city.

African maybe, or West Indian.
Just stumbled out of childhood, staring
10   Into a blank unknown,
And quite unfearing.

I never thought before
So quicksilver a wisp could stay so still
So separate, until
15   What I wished not to see I saw—
Her small black-kitten life was maimed and hobbled;
She leant on crutches; the girl was crippled.

Three times a loser, then.
Her childhood lost, and nothing else begun;
20   Lost too the Caribbean sun;
And half her strength and proper lightness gone.

Yet in her face among that grey-faced crowd
The three lost suns still glowed.

GRAHAM HOUGH

1. Considering *separately* each word of the last line except 'The', show
   the significance of each for the rest of the poem.
2. What do words denoting colour contribute to the poem?
3. Comment on:
   (*a*) muzzle, line 5.
   (*b*) stumbled, line 9.
   (*c*) black-kitten, line 16.
   (*d*) the grammatical structure of line 15.
   (*e*) the use of rhyme.

Grouped nightly at the cold, accepted wall,
Carved with a gaslight chisel the lean heads
Cry out unwittingly for Rembrandt's needle.
These are the flashy saplings whose domain
5   I cannot enter.
They burn at lip and finger the stuffed paper;
The trouser-pocket boys, the cocky walkers,
Sons of old mothers, with their hats askew
Hummock the shoulder to the little flower
10   That lights the palm into a nightmare land,
A bloody basin of the sterile moon,
That lights the face that sprouts the cigarette
Into a sudden passion of fierce colour.
Down the cold corridor of winter nights
15   I see a thousand groups that keep
The fag alight, at walls, and in the sharp
Stern corners of the street:
These are the sprigs; flash boys, uncaught,
Treading the reedy springboard of green days.
20   Theirs is a headiness for they
Have burned their lives up to the quarter-mark.
The days move by them and the chill nights hold them
In an old, unthought conspiracy for they
Tinkle upon tin feet that send no root.
25   I see them at the cold, accepted wall,
The trouser-pocket boys, the cocky walkers.

MERVYN PEAKE

1. The poet structures the poem through images of smoking and images
   of growth in nature. How, through these, does he show the kind of
   life of the youths?
2. What is the relationship between the poet and the youths, and by
   what means does he express it?
3. Get as much as you can out of line 11.
4. Comment on:
   (a) accepted, lines 1 and 25.   (c) Tinkle upon tin feet, line 24.
   (b) quarter-mark, line 21.   (d) the absence of rhyme.

Note: The whole poem is a prayer to God. Below are verses 4–7.

> When frae my mither's womb I fell,
> Thou might hae plung'd me deep in Hell,
> To gnash my gooms, to weep and wail
> 　　　In burnin' lakes,
5
> Whare damnéd devils roar and yell,
> 　　　Chain'd to their stakes.

> Yet I am here, a chosen sample,
> To show thy grace is great and ample;
> I'm here a pillar o' Thy temple,
10
> 　　　Strong as a rock,
> A guide, a buckler, an example
> 　　　To a' Thy flock!

> O Lord, thou kens what zeal I bear,
> When drinkers drink, and swearers swear,
15
> And singin' there and dancin' here,
> 　　　Wi' great and sma':
> For I am keepit by thy fear
> 　　　Free frae them a'.

> But yet, O Lord! confess I must,
20
> At times I'm fash'd wi' fleshly lust;
> An' sometimes, too, in wardly trust,
> 　　　Vile self gets in;
> But Thou remembers we are dust,
> 　　　Defil'd wi' sin.

ROBERT BURNS

1. What are the hypocrisies of the speaker and how does the poet bring them into focus?
2. Show how the poet uses the tone and language of prayer for humorous effect.
3. Get as much as you can out of lines 17, 18.
4. Comment on:

　　(*a*) fell, line 1.　　　　　　(*c*) pillar of thy temple, line 9.
　　(*b*) to gnash my gooms, line 3.　　(*d*) vile self, line 22.

Who'd stoop to blame
This sort of trifling? Even had you skill
In speech—(which I have not)—to make your will
Quite clear to such as one, and say, 'Just this
5   Or that in you disgusts me; here you miss,
Or there exceed the mark'—and if she let
Herself be lessoned so, nor plainly set
Her wits to yours, forsooth, and made excuse,
—E'en then would be some stooping; and I choose
10   Never to stoop. Oh sir, she smiled, no doubt,
Whene'er I passed her; but who passed without
Much the same smile? This grew; I gave commands
Then all smiles stopped together. There she stands
As if alive. Will't please you rise? We'll meet
15   The company below, then. I repeat,
The Count your master's known munificence
Is ample warrant that no just pretence
Of mine for dowry will be disallowed;
Though his fair daughter's self, as I avowed
20   At starting, is my object. Nay, we'll go
Together down, sir. Notice Neptune, though
Taming a sea-horse, thought a rarity,
Which Claus of Innsbruck cast in bronze for me!

ROBERT BROWNING

Note: You should read the whole poem, of which this is the last part before you attempt the questions.

1. Taking 'Will't please you rise?' as the pivot of the two parts of the excerpt, contrast what comes before with what comes after. Think of:

    (*a*) themes
    (*b*) attitude shown by the Duke
    (*c*) tone
    (*d*) grammatical structuring
    (*e*) intonation and rhythm.

2. Talk about the poet's handling of the verse form, the heroic couplet.

Thanks

You never did so much
As when you nearly died;
As if you nearly died
That I might show I lived.

5   That was no more your motive
Than it could have been my choice.
You cannot think I live
Just to give voice!

It was no poet's need you met,
10   And now survive,
But the need I had as a man
To know myself alive.

You never did so much
As when you nearly died;
15   You had to nearly die
For me to know I lived.

DONALD DAVIE

1. What situation gave rise to the poem, what conflict did it bring about, and how was the conflict resolved?
2. Why do you think the poet repeated the first two lines as the opening of the last verse?
3. Comment on:
   (a) the absence of imagery
   (b) the lack of descriptive words
   (c) the use of logical connectives
   (d) only monosyllabic and disyllabic words
   (e) the constant use of 'you' and 'I'.

Clownlike, happiest on your hands,
Feet to the stars, and moon-skulled,
Gilled like a fish. A common-sense
Thumbs-down on the dodo's mode.
5 Wrapped up in yourself like a spool,
Trawling your dark as owls do.
Mute as a turnip from the Fourth
Of July to All Fools' Day,
O high-riser, my little loaf.

10 Vague as fog and looked for like mail.
Farther off than Australia.
Bent-backed Atlas, our travelled prawn.
Snug as a bud and at home
Like a sprat in a pickle jug.
15 A creel of eels, all ripples.
Jumpy as a Mexican bean.
Right, like a well-done sum.
A clean slate, with your own face on.

SYLVIA PLATH

1. The clue to the title is in lines 7 and 8. What is she talking about?
2. There is a finite verb in the title, but no finite verb in the poem. What is the connection between the two?
3. Discuss the imagery of the animate and inanimate worlds.
4. Choose two of the images you find most amusing. Why are they funny, and are they only funny?
5. Look carefully at the recurrences of sound and consider them in relation to the theme.
6. Get as much as you can out of

from the Fourth
of July to All Fool's Day

remembering that Sylvia Plath was an American by birth, domiciled in England.

i thank You God for most this amazing
day: for the leaping greenly spirits of trees
and a blue true dream of sky; and for everything
which is natural which is infinite which is yes

5 (i who have died am alive again today,
and this is the sun's birthday; this is the birth
day of life and of love and wings: and of the gay
great happening illimitably earth)

how should tasting touching hearing seeing
10 breathing any—lifted from the no
of all nothing—human merely being
doubt unimaginable You?

(now the ears of my ears awake and
now the eyes of my eyes are opened)

                                        e. e. cummings

1. Describe the initial experience that gave rise to the poem and the
   poet's presentation of it.
2. What developed from the first experience?
3. Comment on the effects obtained by the unusual syntax in the third
   verse, and on the use of 'yes' in line 4 and 'no' in line 10.
4. Comment on:

     (a) greenly, line 2.
     (b) blue true, line 3.
     (c) illimitably, line 8.
     (d) the last two lines.

The people along the sand
All turn and look one way.
They turn their back on the land.
They look at the sea all day.

5   As long as it takes to pass
A ship keeps raising its hull;
The wetter ground like glass
Reflects a standing gull.

The land may vary more;
10   But wherever the truth may be—
The water comes ashore,
And the people look at the sea.

They cannot look out far.
They cannot look in deep.
15   But when was that ever a bar
To any watch they keep?

ROBERT FROST

1. The poet describes the actions of a particular set of people. What are the actions?
2. By interpreting the symbolic meaning of the last verse give any symbolic meanings you can to the actions.
3. Discuss the various simplifying devices used by the poet to make the symbolism become clear.

At 12 o'clock the Devil is coming to claim Faustus' soul.
Faustus speaks

Ah, Faustus,
Now hast thou but one bare hour to live,
And then thou must be damned perpetually!
Stand still, you ever-moving spheres of Heaven,
5   That time may cease, and midnight never come.
Fair Nature's eye, rise, rise again and make
Perpetual day; or let this hour be but
A year, a month, a week, a natural day,
That Faustus may repent and save his soul!
10   O *lente, lente, currite noctis equi!*
The stars move still, time runs, the clock will strike,
The Devil will come, and Faustus must be damned.
O, I'll leap up to my God! Who pulls me down?
See, see where Christ's blood streams in the firmament!
15   One drop would save my soul—half a drop: ah, my Christ!
Ah, rend not my heart for naming of my Christ!
Yet will I call on him: O spare me, Lucifer!—
Where is it now? 'tis gone; and see where God
Stretcheth out his arm, and bends his ireful brows!
20   Mountain and hills come, come and fall on me,
And hide me from the heavy wrath of God!
No! no!
Then will I headlong run into the earth;
Earth gape! O no, it will not harbour me!
25   You stars that reigned at my nativity,
Whose influence hath allotted death and hell,
Now draw up Faustus like a foggy mist
Into the entrails of yon labouring clouds,
That when they vomit forth into the air,
30   My limbs may issue from their smoky mouths,
So that my soul may but ascend to heaven.

MARLOWE

Taking lines 12 and 22 as critical in the movement of Faustus' mind,
trace the ebb and flow of hope, despair and terror, showing the devices
by which the poet accomplishes his purpose.

The Mouth of the Hudson

(For Esther Brooks) ·

A single man stands like a bird-watcher,
and scuffles the pepper and salt snow
from a discarded, gray
Westinghouse Electric cable drum.
He cannot discover America by counting
the chains of condemned freight-trains
from thirty states. They jolt and jar
and junk in the siding below him.
He has trouble with his balance.
His eyes drop,
and he drifts with the wild ice
ticking seaward down the Hudson,
like the blank sides of a jig-saw puzzle.

The ice ticks seaward like a clock.
A Negro toasts
wheat-seeds over the coke-fumes
of a punctured barrel.
Chemical air
sweeps in from New Jersey,
and smells of coffee.

Across the river,
ledges of suburban factories tan
in the sulphur-yellow sun
of the unforgivable landscape.

ROBERT LOWELL

One duck stood on my toes.
The others made watery rushes after bread
Thrown by my momentary hand; instead,
She stood duck-still and got far more than those.

An invisible drone boomed by
With a beetle in it; the neighbour's yearning bull
Bugled across five fields. And an evening full
Of other evenings quietly began to die.

And my everlasting hand
Dropped on my hypocrite duck her grace of bread.
And I thought, 'The first to be fattened, the first to be
                                    dead',
Till my gestures enlarged, wide over the darkening
                                    land.

NORMAN MCCAIG

Music, when soft voices die,
Vibrates in the memory—
Odours, when sweet violets sicken,
Live within the sense they quicken.

Rose leaves, when the rose is dead,
Are heaped for the beloved's bed;
And so thy thoughts, when thou art gone,
Love itself shall slumber on.

P. B. SHELLEY

Slow moves the acid breath of noon
over the copper-coated hill,
slow from the wild crab's bearded breast
the palsied apples fall.

Like coloured smoke the day hangs fire,
taking the village without sound;
the vulture-headed sun lies low
chained to the violet ground.

The horse upon the rocky height
rolls all the valley in his eye,
but dares not raise his foot or move
his shoulder from the fly.

The sheep, snail-backed against the wall,
lifts her blind face but does not know
the cry her blackened tongue gives forth
is the first bleat of snow.

Each bird and stone, each roof and well,
feels the gold foot of autumn pass;
each spider binds with glittering snare
the splintered bones of grass.

Slow moves the hour that sucks our life,
slow drops the late wasp from the flower,
the rose tree's thread of scent draws thin—
and snaps upon the air.

LAURIE LEE

With snakes of rubber and glass thorax,
like dragons rampant,
statistical, red with ambush,
they ambuscade the highway.

Only in the hinterland, and for neighbours,
the extant blacksmith drives
archaic nails into the three-legged horse.

But on Route 7
the monsters coil and spit from iron mouths
potent saliva.

(Beyond the hills, of course;
the oxen, lyric with horns, still draw
the cart and the limping wheels.)

A. M. KLEIN

I see you did not try to save
The bouquet of white flowers I gave;
So fast they wither on your grave.

Why does it hurt the heart to think
Of that most bitter abrupt brink
Where the low-shouldered coffins sink?

These living bodies that we wear
So change by every seventh year
That in a new dress we appear;

Limbs, spongy brain and slogging heart,
No part remains the selfsame part;
Like streams they stay and still depart.

You slipped slow bodies in the past;
Then why should we be so aghast
You flung off the whole flesh at last?

Let him who loves you think instead
That like a woman who has wed
You undressed first and went to bed.

ANDREW YOUNG